ENDOMORPH COOKBOOK

COMPLETE GUIDE

The presentation of the information is without a contract or any type of guarantee assurance.

The information herein is offered for informational purposes solely and is universal as so. The presentation of the information is without contract or any type of guarantee assurance. Readers acknowledge that the author is not engaging in the rendering of legal, financial, medical or professional advice. Please consult a licensed professional before attempting any techniques outlined in this book.

Table of Content

Introduction

Body type, or somatotype, refers to the idea that there are certain generalized body compositions that people are predetermined to have.

In the 1940s, American researcher and psychologist William Sheldon classified different body types into three main groups:

- Ectomorphic
- Mesomorphic
- Endomorphic

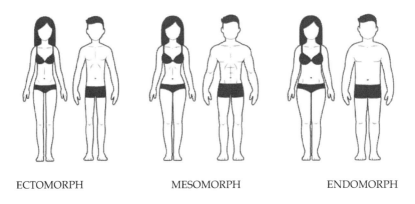

ECTOMORPH   MESOMORPH   ENDOMORPH

His classification was based on the skeletal frame and body composition, which is mainly inherited by our ancestors. We could be leaner, heavier or somewhere in the middle, our bodies could be composed of more muscle tissue and less fat or vice versa.

Because each individual body is composed and works a little different than others, weight loss and general body figure goals require individualized diet program. That's where we step in.

This book is devoted to endomorphic body type. Whether you're looking for ways to easily drop extra pounds or would just want to shape your body figure with some muscle, this book might be the one for you.

In the following chapters, you will get to know all about endomorphic body type. We prepared for you the most efficient diet and exercise regime, along with a 4-week diet plan and a 4-week exercise plan, to help you plan your meals ahead and thus stay on track with the diet. You can also find 111 delishes and easy to make recipes in this book, to spice up your diet and help you become healthier and more energetic.

ENDOMORPHIC BODY TYPE

According to research, endomorphic people have a higher percentage of body fat and lower percentage of muscle tissue in their bodies. This is why they usually look rounder and thicker, with a larger frame and curvy hips and thigs, even though this does not mean they are necessarily obese. Having that said, most of heavily overweight or obese people nonetheless belongs to an endomorph body type group.

The biggest problem of an endomorph is that their body, with its slow metabolism, makes extremely good use of all the food it ingests and stores it quickly in the form of fat: both subcutaneous and internal fat that surrounds the organs. In comparison to other body types, endomorphs are more sensitive to calorie consumption. They must constantly watch what they eat, to ensure they do not eat more than they burn and consequently, gain weight.

Endomorph can also have problems relying on the scales, as minor dietary adjustments can lead to some weight loss, but mostly the lost pounds represent lost water that endomorphs often retain in their body.

If an endomorph combines above predispositions with a sedentary lifestyle and poor dietary choices, he may quickly find himself in a situation where he will have to tackle his excess weight problems for health reasons, not just for aesthetic reasons.

The good news is that endomorphs mostly gain muscle mass quite easily, which can help them fight their higher percentage of body fat. In order to do so, endomorphs really need to put extra effort into body shaping and combine an individualized diet along with an exercise plan. Just a general workout and diet advise might not work for them.

In comparison with endomorphs, people with an ectomorph body type have better and more efficient metabolisms, which results in eating more and gaining less (or even no additional) weight. Their body size is, in general, smaller and their frame narrower. To sum up: ectomorphs look very thin with almost no fat or muscle. You probably have a friend, a co-worker or even a family member, who is very skinny, despite eating a lot, who never counts calories (even when snacking) and doesn't put on any weight? This might seem impossible to an endomorph.

The mesomorph body type is, as evident from the name itself, somewhere in between the endomorph and ectomorphic type. People who have mesomorph body types have a larger skeletal frame than ectomorphs, but a lower percentage of body fat than endomorphs. They look athletic and have more muscle tissue so when dieting, they have no troubles shaping their body figure with muscle and lose weight easily.

The general theory is, that all people can be divided into the above mentioned three main groups of body types: endomorphic, ectomorphic or mesomorphic type. Of course, this is not always the case, as the categories are generalized and some people might feel they are somewhere in between. In order to be completely sure, it is advisable to assess one's exact body type by taking into account some objective measurements, for example, the amount of fat and muscle mass a person has.

Even though many people think, that endomorph body type is not ideal, all hope is not loss. This book holds just the right tactics for any endomorph to lose weight, get in shape in become healthy.

WHAT IS AN ENDOMORPH DIET?

The endomorph diet is an eating plan, which has been developed and individualized especially for endomorphs. Due to a higher percentage of body fat and lower percentage of muscle tissue in an endomorphs body, endomorph diet plan focuses primarily on fat loss.

Several factors are important while on the endomorph diet, but it will probably not be an exaggeration to say that the most important thing is the frequency of meals. Since meals should be frequent, they should also be small. This is because an endomorph has to deal with his slow metabolism, and this can only be tackled by constantly employing it. It is important to do it as often as possible.

In contrary to most other diets, the endomorph diet does not limit the number of calories a person consumes per day. It does recommend a somewhat equal split of macronutrients, which means you should eat approx. 35 percent protein, 30 percent carbohydrates, and 35 percent fats. This division is, however, not the standard diet of an average Americans, as they usually consume almost 50 percent carbs, only 15 percent protein, and approx. 35 percent fat during a regular day.

However, if you want to achieve weight loss while on endomorph diet, your daily intake of calories should still be in deficit, in comparison whit what you burn out. So, it is nonetheless important to keep a track of the ratio, for optimal results.

When on endomorph diet plan, the choice of nutrients is very important. An endomorph must always eat a meal that will be in line with his activities until the next meal. For example, he should eat energy-rich foods if he planes to do some activities throughout the day, and rather go for a protein or fiber rich dinner.

Keep in mind that lives of endomorphs will be much easier by eating large amounts of lower energy food. Larger volumes of food will keep them full. Foods with lower energy value (food with little and unsaturated fat, protein, foods with lots of fiber, vegetable, etc.) will increase their metabolism and keep their body happy and healthy.

Sugar, alcohol, white flour products (bread, pastries, noodles, etc.), highly processed foods (including fast food) and foods high in fat are unsuitable for endomorph's metabolism as such foods slows the metabolism down and could cause constipation. To sum up, the endomorph diet encourages eating more protein, fiber, and healthy fats while lowering carb and intake.

The endomorph diet plan can also boost strength and help with the growth of muscle, which helps define your body figure. The diet plan itself is thus not only for those who want to lose some weight, but also for those who just want to look great and follow a healthy, balanced and nutritious diet.

Overall, endomorphs are in general good eaters, but they shouldn't eat too much. Portioning of meals is of great importance. This does not apply only for endomorph diet, but to all diets out there.

WHAT TO EAT?

Endomorphs should focus on healthy, whole-food sources of protein and healthy fat such as fish, lean meat (skinless chicken or turkey and red meat, such as beef, lamb and even pork with the fat trimmed off, if necessary), eggs, beans, avocado, nuts, coconuts, olive oil and other unrefined and cold press vegetable oils (avocado oil, peanut oil, coconut oil, etc.).

A good protein source might also represent low fat dairy products (milk, yoghurt, etc.) along with cheese. In addition, vegan types of milk and yogurt are allowed as they are usually not rich in fat or sugar and contain a lot of fiber. They are also a great substitute for people who are lactose intolerant.

There are a few things an endomorph should know about fat. Healthy fat is reach in omega-3 fatty acids. It can be found, for example, in nuts, fish, butter along with its better version: ghee butter, olives and avocados. On the other hand, unhealthy fat sources can be found in margarine, heavily processed food and oils and fatty meat. Some of the oils you should avoid, since they are nowadays highly processed and not cold pressed, are: canola, soybean, sunflower, and corn oil.

Unhealthy fat, on the other hand, is rich in omega-6 fatty acids and is harmful to your body. The consumption of larger quantities of unhealthy fat over long periods of time usually causes chronic inflammation as well as high cholesterol levels. This impacts your weight, but more importantly, your heart health and bad cholesterol levels. In comparison, eating healthy fat (omega-3 fatty acids) has no harmful effect on your body and can even have positively affect your health, by increasing the healthy cholesterol levels in your blood and helping with absorption of vitamins A, K and other fat-soluble vitamins.

Endomorphs don't have to cut out carbs completely. They should rather lower the amount of carbs they usually eat, to 30 or less percent per daily intake. Removing carbs from your diet can trigger sluggishness and fatigue. If too extreme, a low-carb diet can also lead to gastrointestinal problems and ketosis. Not all carbs are bad for your body, if you choose the right sources, there are many health benefits for you and are a great energy source.

Focus on complex carbohydrates. For example, vegetables, sweet potatoes, oats, berries, and legumes are all great carbohydrate options. Other complex carbohydrate options include flakes, bran and fullgrain four products. Make sure to limit an intake of simple carbohydrates, for example, white bread, white rice, pasta, cakes, pastries, and cookies. Simple carbohydrates are high in sugar and calories, which can lead to fat storage and can increase your blood sugar.

In addition, carbs are recommended to eat after the daily workout or activities, as this is when your body uses them to replenish and build muscles, not store fat.

Sugar (including sweetened beverages, sweets, pastries, etc.), unrefined or not, should usually be avoided as it slows down metabolism and can cause constipation. It can be used, though, in smaller quantities and not as an everyday snack.

Sugar can cause addiction over time, moreover eating sugary foods leaves cravings throughout the day and can cause weight gain, binge eating, low energy levels and bad skin. It is also linked to some heart diseases. A good option is to use natural sweeteners instead of raw sugar, like honey.

Another group of food you should avoid is industrially processed food. This means no chips, crackers, biscuits, granola, fast food, etc. Certainly, avoidance of processed foods is of great importance for improving a person's health and well-being, as there is far too much of this on the plate these days.

Processed food also includes other unhealthy ingredients such as artificial colorings, flavorings, preservatives, and other industrial additives. To ease your dieting, this book contains a lot of healthy recipes for alternatives to processed food, which are healthy for you.

Among unsuitable products to consume when practicing an endomorph diet is also alcohol. Similar to sugar and industrially processed food, it slows down an endomorph's metabolism and could cause constipation. In addition, some types of alcohol are full of carbohydrates (for example, beer), and some are full of sugar (sweet vines, sweet liqueurs, etc.). This however, does not mean, that you can't enjoy a glass of dry wine then and there. Just try to limit the quantities to a minimum.

Fruit is a healthy addition to an endomorph diet, as well as to any other type of diet. It contains a lot of vitamins, minerals and fiber and is good for your health. If you're sensitive to carbohydrates, eat fruit in moderation or choose fruit with lower glycemic index or less sugar (berries, green apples, grapefruit, strawberries, cherries, plums, etc.).

Last but not least, always choose organic food options. Go to a local market and try to get to know where your food comes from. Talk to the farmers and let them tell you which fruit or veggies are ripe and in season. Always buy and eat food that is in season. Seasonal food is fresher and tastes better, it contains a lot more nutrients and flavor than prepackaged food and does not need any additives to help with the flavor or ripens. It is also very natural for your body and will have the best health effects for you.

When picking out fish, try to buy fish low in mercury. Some options include pollock, sardines, salmon, tilapia, oysters, shrimps, clams and crabs.

As regards the meat, eggs and dairy products, always choose products, coming from a grass fed or a free-range animal. These types of food include as little additives as possible, or even no additives at all. Such food is usually ecological and animal friendly. By buying a grass fed or a free-range animal product, you will also encourage and support the farmers who are struggling to provide its customers with the best quality food.

ARE THERE ANY DOWNSIDES?

As already mentioned in the above chapters, there are many positive effects of the endomorph diet to a person's overall health. Not only will it help manage you weight (or lose some, if you wish), it will also help you shape your body figure, by transferring some of your fat tissue to muscle tissue.

Since the diet encourages you to eat healthy and nutritious food, like vegetable, protein, healthy fat and fruit on one hand, and discourages you to eat unhealthy fat, sugary, greasy food and highly processed food on the other hand, this will greatly contribute to your heart and gut health. In addition, it will help reduce inflammation, regulate your blood sugar and improve the health of your internal organs.

The diet itself isn't harmful, as you are encouraged to eat healthy food options and you can still eat all groups of food – even though some, like carbs, in limited quantities. Nonetheless, there are some downsides and concerns you should address prior to starting the diet.

- If you have any underlying medical conditions, it is important to consult your doctor before changing your current diet.
- The diet might be complicated to follow from the beginning, depending on what your current diet looks like. There are several rules on what to eat and what not, so following them can be a needlessly tough way to lose weight.
- The diet highlights a lot of fresh ingredients and sustainably sourced animal products. While these foods are definitely better for your health in the long run, they are usually more expensive.
- Body type descriptions and definitions might be oversimplified. Recognizing your body type can be difficult and you might feel that it lacks individualization. It not only depends on the shape of your

body, but is impacted of many different factors including your genetics, food choices, average physical activity, stress, amount of sleep, your choice of job, family and social support, etc. In order for an endomorph diet to be successful, you will probably have to make changes in almost all those aspects. This might be hard on you and might take a lot of time and effort to achieve.

- The ratio of muscle and fat isn't the only consideration for determining metabolism as metabolism takes into account a multitude of components such as your musculoskeletal system along with your hormones and genetics. But the general rule still applies: the more muscle you have, the faster your metabolism will work and vice versa.

In any case, if you use the diet properly, stick to the rules and make sure you eat quality types of food while regularly exercising, you should be just fine. So, if you're interested in exploring the endomorph diet, this book might be just right for you.

HOW TO USE THE BOOK

The book consists of the following parts:

- general diet guide,
- a cookbook, containing 111 healthy and delicious recipes,
- a four-week diet plan and
- a four-week exercise pan.

First part of the book, is purposed to generally outline the idea and basic principles of the endomorph diet. By reading it, you will get to know what endomorph diet is, what to eat and what not and in what ratio. You will also learn about the benefits ad downsides of the diet.

In the second part of the book, you will find 111 healthy and delicious recipes for breakfast, lunch, dinner and everyday snacks. The presented dishes only contain ingredients, which you are encouraged to eat while practicing the diet. By each recipe, you can find useful information about nutrition as well as tips and tricks for preparation. Nutrition information consist of two important information. First, it shows how many calories and grams of each type of nutrients you consumed. This information is calculated per serving. Furthermore, it also shows percentage of intake, by some of the nutrients you consumed, which is calculated per your daily intake. This way, you will have at most control of what type of and how many nutrients you are consuming by every meal.

You can combine the recipes however you wish, having in mind that through an individual meal or day by day, you should follow the general endomorph ratio: 35% protein, 30 % carbs and 35% fat.

The third part of the book consists of a four-week diet plan. You can find the recipes for each of the dishes in the recipe part of the book. It will help you plan your meals ahead and lose your excess weight easily. You can always come back to this meal plan, if you ever feel like you cheated on the diet too much or you wish to lose some extra pounds.

The last part of the book is dedicated to training and exercise. You will find therein a 4-week exercise plan with tricks and tips, which is the most efficient for an endomorph body type. By exercising regularly, you will lose extra fat tissue and transfer it to muscle.

For a diet to be successful, you need to devote a lot of time into planning and preparing meals. It is easier if you have some experience with cooking.

Depending on your current diet, it is advisable to slowly change your regular diet, especially so if you are a beginner. This way, you will slowly prepare your body for a change, instead of rushing into a severe change of daily diet instantly.

Don't feel bad if you cheat on the diet every now and then. And most importantly, do not cut out something you really love to eat. This usually backfires and can get you out of a healthy track. Try to enjoy the journey and be creative!

Bon appetite!

COOKBOOK

1. BREAKFAST RECIPES

COCONUT GRANOLA

Prep time: 10 min	Cook time: 2 hours	Servings: 4

Ingredients

- *2 cup raw walnuts*
- *1 cup pumpkin seeds*
- *1 cup flaked coconut, unsweetened*
- *2 tbsp flax seeds*
- *1/4 cup maple syrup*
- *1/3 cup coconut oil*
- *2 tsp vanilla extract*
- *1/2 tsp sea salt*

Instructions

- Soak the walnuts and pumpkin seeds in water with a pinch of salt overnight or about 8 hours. Soaking nuts first removes enzyme inhibitors, making them easier to digest.
- Preheat the oven to 250 ° F.
- Drain the nuts, rinse and dry with a cloth. Cut the nuts into small pieces or chunks or place the nuts in the bowl of a food processor and press briefly until coarsely chopped. I cut them so that not all nuts are the same size for variety, but do whatever you want!
- In a large bowl, combine the chopped nuts, dried coconut, chia seeds and cocoa powder. Add maple syrup, melted coconut oil, vanilla extract and sea salt and stir until all dry ingredients are completely covered with wet ingredients.
- Place the granola on a parchment-lined baking sheet and bake for about 2 1/2 to 3 hours, stirring every half hour.

NUTRITION FACTS (PER SERVING)

Calories	773	
Total Fat	62.5g	80%
Saturated Fat	14.7g	74%
Cholesterol	0mg	0%
Sodium	248mg	11%
Total Carbohydrate	38.9g	14%
Dietary Fiber	13g	46%
Total Sugars	16.6g	
Protein	24.8g	

Tips: You can use any nuts which one your choice like almonds, cashew, Hazelnuts, Brazil nuts, etc.

HEALTHY EGG BREAKFAST MUFFINS

Prep time: 5 min	Cook time: 20 min	Servings: 8

Ingredients

- *8 eggs*
- *1 cup cauliflower (diced)*
- *1 cup onion (diced)*
- *1/2 cup spinach*
- *1 tsp garlic (minced)*
- *1 cup diced mushrooms*
- *salt and pepper, to taste*

Instructions

- Preheat the oven to 350° F.
- Cut all the vegetables into cubes.

- In a large bowl, combine the eggs, vegetables, salt and pepper.
- To mix in a greased muffin pan, the mixture should fill 8 muffin bowls evenly.
- Bake for 18 to 20 minutes.
- Serve warm.

NUTRITION FACTS (PER SERVING)

Calories	75	
Total Fat	4.4g	6%
Saturated Fat	1.4g	7%
Cholesterol	164mg	55%
Sodium	68mg	3%
Total Carbohydrate	2.8g	1%
Dietary Fiber	0.8g	3%
Total Sugars	1.4g	
Protein	6.3g	

Tips: The muffins puff up while they cook in the oven. Fill them 3/4 of the way up to prevent overflow

ZUCCHINI BREAD

Prep time: 10 min	Cook time: 35 min	Servings: 8

Ingredients

- 1 1/2 cups coconut flour
- 1 1/2 tsp baking soda
- 1/2 tsp salt
- 1 tsp nutmeg
- 1 cup grated zucchini (squeezed)
- 3 eggs
- 3 tbsp honey
- 1/2 cup applesauce
- 1 tbsp melted coconut oil

Instructions

- Preheat the oven to 350° F and line a pan with parchment paper.
- In a large bowl, whisk the dry ingredients together.
- Add the wet ingredients except the zucchini and beat until well combined.
- Add the zucchini and stir until just combined.
- Beat in a loaf pan lined with parchment paper.
- Bake for about 35 minutes, until the top is golden and the center of the loaf is firm.
- Take out of the oven and let cool in the pan for 10 minutes.
- Remove the bread from the pan by pulling the sides of the parchment paper and return it to the wire rack to cool completely before slicing.

NUTRITION FACTS (PER SERVING)

Calories	79	
Total Fat	3.3g	4%
Saturated Fat	1.4g	7%
Cholesterol	61mg	20%
Sodium	424mg	18%
Total Carbohydrate	10.5g	4%
Dietary Fiber	1.4g	5%
Total Sugars	8.7g	
Protein	2.7g	

Tips: NEVER peel your zucchini for zucchini bread, it contains nutrients, and gives the bread added texture and flavor.

STRAWBERRY PANCAKE

Prep time: 10 min	Cook time: 35 min	Servings: 6

Ingredients

- *1 1/2 cups finely coconut flour*
- *2 eggs*
- *1/2 tsp cinnamon*
- *1/2 tsp nutmeg*
- *1/2 cup pureed strawberries*
- *1/4 tsp baking powder*
- *1/4 cup coconut milk*
- *olive oil for frying*

Instructions

- Mix all the ingredients except olive oil for frying.
- Put the olive oil in a saucepan and heat until melted.
- Use 1/4 cup of batter to prepare each pancake.
- Fry until golden brown on each side.
- Garnish with more mashed strawberries.

NUTRITION FACTS (PER SERVING)		
Calories	189	
Total Fat	9.3g	12%
Saturated Fat	4.9g	25%
Cholesterol	55mg	18%
Sodium	22mg	1%
Total Carbohydrate	21.9g	8%
Dietary Fiber	12.6g	45%
Total Sugars	1.1g	
Protein	6.2g	

Tips: While it might be tempting to cook your pancakes on your regular, round pan, a flat griddle will have much more room for cooking and flipping your pancakes.

BREAKFAST BARS WITH STRAWBERRY

Prep time: 10 min	Cook time: 35 min	Servings: 10

Ingredients

- *1 1/2 cups almond, chopped*
- *1 1/2 cups unsweetened coconut flakes*
- *2 ripe bananas*
- *1 tsp vanilla*
- *1/2 tsp salt*
- *strawberry jam*

Instructions

- Preheat the oven to 350 degrees. Line the loaf pan with parchment paper. Put a cup of nuts and a cup of coconut flakes in a food processor. Impulse to decompose. Add the bananas, vanilla and salt and mix until the mixture is completely combined. Transfer the mixture to a loaf pan and use a spatula to smooth. Bake for 25 minutes.

- In the meantime, put the remaining coconut flakes in a saucepan over medium heat. Roast until lightly browned, stirring frequently. Remove the stove. Add the remaining nuts.
- Take the bread pan out of the oven and spread a thin layer of jam on the bars. Sprinkle the mixture of toasted coconut flakes on top. Bake another 5 to 10 minutes or until golden brown. Let cool completely before cutting into bars. Refrigerate 30 minutes before serving. Keep refrigerated.

NUTRITION FACTS (PER SERVING)

Calories	215	
Total Fat	16.8g	22%
Saturated Fat	9g	45%
Cholesterol	0mg	0%
Sodium	123mg	5%
Total Carbohydrate	12.7g	5%
Dietary Fiber	4.8g	17%
Total Sugars	4.7g	
Protein	4.5g	

Tips: Almonds contain a lot of healthy fats, fiber, protein and magnesium. Eating them helps lowering blood sugar levels, reducing blood pressure and lowering cholesterol levels.

MUSHROOM OMELET

Prep time: 10 min	Cook time: 25 min	Servings: 4

Ingredients

- 6 large eggs
- 1/2 cup almond milk
- 1/4 cup fresh mushrooms, sliced
- 1/4 cup bell pepper, sliced
- 1/2 onion sliced
- 1 tbsp fresh parsley, minced
- sea salt and freshly ground black pepper to taste

Instructions

- Preheat your oven to 350 F.

- Beat the eggs in a bowl with the almond milk and season with sea salt and black pepper.
- Pour the eggs into a round saucepan or cake pan and distribute the rest of the ingredients on top.
- Place in the oven and bake for 20-25 minutes.

NUTRITION FACTS (PER SERVING)

Calories	38	
Total Fat	0.4g	1%
Saturated Fat	0g	0%
Cholesterol	0mg	0%
Sodium	166mg	7%
Total Carbohydrate	2.3g	1%
Dietary Fiber	0.2g	1%
Total Sugars	1.6g	
Protein	5.8g	

Tips: Beat the eggs well until no more flecks of white can be seen. It should be frothy and light.

STRAWBERRY DONUTS

Prep time: 30 min	Cook time: 20 min	Servings: 12

Ingredients

- *4 large eggs, room temperature*
- *3 tbsp coconut oil melted*
- *1/2 cup almond milk, warm*
- *1/4 cup maple syrup*
- *1 tsp apple cider vinegar*
- *1 tsp pure vanilla extract*
- *1/2 cup almond flour*
- *1/4 cup freeze dried strawberries, ground to a powder*
- *1/2 tsp baking soda*
- *1/4 tsp sea salt*

Instructions

- Preheat a donut maker. If using a donut pan, preheat the oven to 350F and generously grease the pan with butter or ghee.
- Using a stand mixer or electric hand mixer, beat eggs with coconut oil on medium to high speed until creamy.
- Add milk, maple syrup, vinegar and vanilla and beat again until combined.
- Sift the remaining dry ingredients into the bowl using a fine mesh sieve or colander. Beat over high heat until smooth.
- Place the dough in a large Ziplock bag, seal the top, and cut off one of the bottom corners.
- Pour the batter into the donut pan and fill it completely.
- Bake until the light on the donut maker goes out or bake for approx. 17 minutes in a pan. Remove the donuts and let them cool on a wire rack. Cut if necessary.

NUTRITION FACTS (PER SERVING)

Calories	114	
Total Fat	8.6g	11%
Saturated Fat	3.7g	18%
Cholesterol	62mg	21%
Sodium	138mg	6%
Total Carbohydrate	6.8g	2%
Dietary Fiber	0.9g	3%
Total Sugars	4.9g	
Protein	3.4g	

Tips: before glazing, frosting, and filling, make sure that your doughnuts are completely cool so that nothing melts!

OVERNIGHT GRAIN FREE OATS

Prep time: 30 min	Cook time: 20 min	Servings: 12

Ingredients

- 3 tbsp flax seeds
- 1/2 tbsp coconut flour
- 2 tbsp vanilla protein powder
- 2 tsp chia seeds
- 2/3 cup almond milk
- a sprinkle of nutmeg
- toppings: fresh berries, cacao nibs, coconut and/or almond butter

Instructions

- Place all the ingredients except the garnish in a mason jar. Stir until everything is well combined.
- Cover with a lid and refrigerate overnight (or at least a few hours) to thicken.
- Take out of the fridge, add milk if necessary, stir and sprinkle over the ingredients.

NUTRITION FACTS (PER SERVING)

Calories	668	
Total Fat	30.3g	39%
Saturated Fat	4.6g	23%
Cholesterol	20mg	7%
Sodium	330mg	14%
Total Carbohydrate	40.9g	15%
Dietary Fiber	29.1g	104%
Total Sugars	3.4g	
Protein	61.4g	

Tips: these oats are a great source of protein and fiber and make a delicious and healthy breakfast or an after-lunch dessert the whole family will enjoy.

KALE OMELETTE

| Prep time: 10 min | Cook time: 15 min | Servings: 2 |

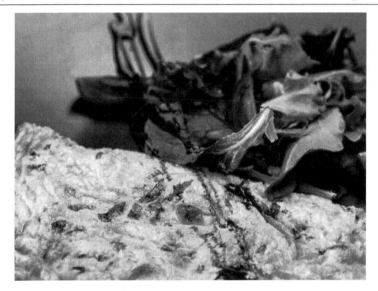

Ingredients

- *4 eggs*
- *1/4 cup kale, chopped*
- *1/2 onion, diced*
- *2 tbsp almond milk*
- *1/4 cup tomatoes, diced*
- *1 green onion, sliced*
- *1 garlic clove, minced*
- *2 tbsp coconut oil*
- *sea salt and freshly ground black pepper*

Instructions

- Melt coconut oil in a skillet over medium to high heat.
- Add the onion and garlic. Cook for 1 to 2 minutes or until tender.
- Add the kale, remove from the heat and mix everything together.
- Break the eggs into a bowl, add the almond milk and season to taste. Beat until everything is well combined.
- In another skillet, melt the remaining oil over medium heat.
- Pour the beaten egg into the pan and cook until it is firm enough to be turned.
- Serve the omelet with diced tomatoes and spring onions.

NUTRITION FACTS (PER SERVING)		
Calories	301	
Total Fat	26g	33%
Saturated Fat	17.7g	88%
Cholesterol	327mg	109%
Sodium	367mg	16%
Total Carbohydrate	6.9g	3%
Dietary Fiber	1.6g	6%
Total Sugars	3.1g	
Protein	12.4g	

Tips: If you use a pan that's too big, your egg will be super-thin and break under the weight of your fillings.

TURKEY STUFFED AVOCADO

Prep time: 10 min	Cook time: 15 min	Servings: 2

Ingredients

- *1 avocado, halved and seeded*
- *1 cup chopped cooked turkey*
- *1/4 cup diced fresh tomato*
- *1 tbsp sour cream*
- *1 tsp whole grain mustard*
- *1 tsp regular mustard*
- *1 tbsp lemon juice*
- *1 tbsp chopped fresh basil*
- *1/4 tsp cayenne pepper*
- *salt and pepper to taste*

Instructions

- Place the turkey, tomato, mustard, sour cream, lemon juice, chopped cilantro and cayenne pepper in a bowl and mix.
- Season to taste with salt and black pepper.
- Pour the mixture into the avocado halves and serve.

NUTRITION FACTS (PER SERVING)		
Calories	388	
Total Fat	28.2g	36%
Saturated Fat	6.1g	30%
Cholesterol	57mg	19%
Sodium	162mg	7%
Total Carbohydrate	13.4g	5%
Dietary Fiber	7.1g	25%
Total Sugars	2.2g	
Protein	22.9g	

Tips: Turkey is a very rich source of protein, niacin, vitamin B6 and the amino acid tryptophane. Apart from these nutrients, it is also containing zinc and vitamin B12.

SMOKED TUNA AVOCADO DEVILED EGGS

Prep time: 15 min	Cook time: 30 min	Servings: 12

Ingredients

- *6 hardboiled eggs*
- *1/4 cup homemade mayo*
- *1 tsp mustard*
- *1 tsp white vinegar*
- *pinch of salt*
- *1 avocado*
- *1 package smoked tuna*
- *small bunch of basil*

Instructions

- Cut the hard-boiled eggs lengthwise and place the hard-boiled yolks in a bowl. Reserve the whites. Combine the mayonnaise, mustard, vinegar and salt in the bowl with the egg yolks. Mix until everything is well incorporated.
- Using a small spoon or a pastry bag, pour the egg yolk mixture into the hollowed-out egg white halves.
- Crush the avocado or cut it into small pieces and place it on the edge of the egg yolk mixture. Cut the smoked salmon into small pieces and place it on the other side of the egg yolk. Garnish with basil

NUTRITION FACTS (PER SERVING)

Calories	86	
Total Fat	6g	8%
Saturated Fat	1.5g	7%
Cholesterol	82mg	27%
Sodium	90mg	4%
Total Carbohydrate	2.1g	1%
Dietary Fiber	1.2g	4%
Total Sugars	0.4g	
Protein	6.5g	

Tips: After boiling your eggs for 10-12 minutes, put them in cold water to bring the temperature down rapidly and stop the cooking process. You can even use ice cubes in your water, and you can change the water as it warms. If you wish to prepare a healthier version of this meal, use sour cream instead of mayo.

AVOCADO FRIES

Prep time: 5 min	Cook time: 10 min	Servings: 12

Ingredients

- *4 tbsp almond flour*
- *1/4 tsp sea or kosher salt*
- *1/4 tsp freshly ground black pepper*
- *2 egg whites*
- *2 firm, ripe avocados*
- *olive oil spray*

Instructions

- Preheat the grill.
- Combine flour, salt and pepper in a shallow bowl. Put the egg white in a small bowl and beat until frothy.

- Cut the avocados in half, remove the bone and cut each half into 6 wedges. Remove the pods.
- Brush the avocado slices with the coconut flour, dip in the egg white and then again in the coconut flour. Take the baking sheet out of the oven. Place the avocado slices on a baking sheet and spray them thoroughly with the olive oil spray.
- Grill for 5 minutes or until golden brown. Flip and grill for another 2 minutes. Devour.

NUTRITION FACTS (PER SERVING)

Calories	203	
Total Fat	18.3g	23%
Saturated Fat	3.4g	17%
Cholesterol	0mg	0%
Sodium	168mg	7%
Total Carbohydrate	8.2g	3%
Dietary Fiber	5.8g	21%
Total Sugars	0.8g	
Protein	4.7g	

Tips: Avocados contain a lot of vitamins (C, E, K, etc.), along with magnesium, potassium and other healthy nutrients.

TORTILLA CHIPS

Prep time: 10 min	Cook time: 10 min	Servings: 2

Ingredients

- 1 1/2 cups blanched almond flour
- 1/2 cup golden flax meal
- 2 egg whites
- 1/2 tsp Celtic sea salt

Instructions

- Put the almond flour, flax flour, egg white and salt in a food processor.
- Mix until a ball of dough forms.
- Divide the dough in half.
- Place each piece of dough between 2 pieces of baking paper.
- Roll out the dough until it is 3/4 inch thick or even thinner.
- Remove the top of the parchment paper.

- Place the bottom of the parchment paper with the rolled dough on the baking sheet.
- Repeat the process with the remaining piece of dough.
- Cut into 2½-inch triangular quarters on each side.
- Bake at 350 ° F for 10 to 12 minutes.

NUTRITION FACTS (PER SERVING)

Calories	100	
Total Fat	7.8g	10%
Saturated Fat	0.6g	3%
Cholesterol	0mg	0%
Sodium	30mg	1%
Total Carbohydrate	3.8g	1%
Dietary Fiber	2.1g	7%
Total Sugars	0g	
Protein	3.8g	

Tips: The tortilla chips will fry better if they are a bit dried out first.

MATCHA CHIA PUDDING WITH BERRIES

| Prep time: 5 min | Cook time: 00 min | Servings: 2 |

Ingredients

- 2 tsp matcha green tea powder
- 1 cup almond milk
- 1/4 cup chia seeds
- 1/2 tablespoon honey
- toppings: raspberries and almonds

Instructions

- In a large bowl, combine the matcha green tea powder with the almond milk and beat until smooth.
- Add the chia seeds and honey. Stir to combine, making sure there are no clumps of chia seeds. Put it in the fridge for 2 hours or overnight.

- Garnish with fresh fruit, muesli and / or nuts.

NUTRITION FACTS (PER SERVING)

Calories	312	
Total Fat	29.7g	38%
Saturated Fat	25.5g	127%
Cholesterol	0mg	0%
Sodium	19mg	1%
Total Carbohydrate	12.5g	5%
Dietary Fiber	4.9g	17%
Total Sugars	8.3g	
Protein	4.4g	

Tips: You can freeze the chia seed pudding for up to 3 months in individual servings. Use freezer-safe zip lock bags or small mason jar containers. To thaw, just place in the fridge overnight.

VEGETABLE FRITTATA

Prep time: 10 min	Cook time: 15 min	Servings: 6

Ingredients

- *2 tbsp coconut oil*
- *1 small green bell pepper, diced*
- *1 small red bell pepper, diced*
- *1 small zucchini, diced*
- *1/2 red onion, thinly sliced*
- *2 cups packed baby kale*
- *¼ cup tomatoes, chopped*
- *1 clove garlic, sliced*
- *10 large eggs, beaten*
- *kosher salt and freshly ground black pepper*

Instructions

- Preheat the oven to 375 ° F.
- Heat oil on a medium nonstick skillet over medium-high heat. Add the bell pepper, zucchini, and onion and cook, stirring occasionally, 6 to 7 minutes, until tender.
- Add the kale, tomatoes and garlic and cook, stirring frequently, for about 1 minute, until the kale is wilted and still bright green.
- Reduce the heat to low and add the eggs, 1 teaspoon of salt and a little ground black pepper. Stir gently to distribute the vegetables. Bake, 13 to 15 minutes, until the eggs are set.
- Let stand 5 minutes then cut into 6 pieces. Serve with hot sauce.

NUTRITION FACTS (PER SERVING)

Calories	64	
Total Fat	4.6g	6%
Saturated Fat	3.9g	20%
Cholesterol	0mg	0%
Sodium	15mg	1%
Total Carbohydrate	5.5g	2%
Dietary Fiber	1g	4%
Total Sugars	1.6g	
Protein	1.4g	

Tip: You can store a frittata in an airtight container in the refrigerator for up to 1 week.

EGGS WITH ASPARAGUS

Prep time: 5 min	Cook time: 10 min	Servings: 2

Ingredients

- *1 pound asparagus*
- *1/2-pint cherry tomatoes*
- *2 eggs*
- *1 tbsp olive oil*
- *1 tsp chopped fresh thyme*
- *salt and pepper to taste*

Instructions

- Preheat the oven to 400 ° F. Grease a baking sheet with nonstick cooking spray or use a baking paper.

- Distribute the asparagus and cherry tomatoes evenly on the baking sheet. Drizzle the vegetables with olive oil. Season to taste with thyme, salt and pepper.
- Roast in the oven until the asparagus is almost tender and the tomatoes are crumpled, 10 to 12 minutes.
- Crack the eggs over the asparagus. Season each with salt and pepper.
- Return to oven and bake until egg whites are set but yolks are still moving, another 7 to 8 minutes.
- To serve, arrange asparagus, tomatoes and eggs on two plates.

NUTRITION FACTS (PER SERVING)

Calories	186	
Total Fat	11.9g	15%
Saturated Fat	2.5g	12%
Cholesterol	164mg	55%
Sodium	71mg	3%
Total Carbohydrate	13g	5%
Dietary Fiber	6g	22%
Total Sugars	7g	
Protein	11.4g	

Tips: Asparagus is a low-calorie vegetable that is an excellent source of essential vitamins and minerals, especially folate and vitamins A, C and K.

GREEN SHAKSHUKA

Prep time: 20 min	Cook time: 15 min	Servings: 4

Ingredients

- *2 tbsp olive oil*
- *1 onion, minced*
- *2 garlic cloves, minced*
- *1 jalapeño, seeded and minced*
- *1-pound kale*
- *1 tsp dried cumin*
- *¾ tsp coriander*
- *salt and freshly ground black pepper*
- *1/2 cup vegetable broth*
- *8 large eggs*
- *chopped fresh parsley for garnish*
- *chopped fresh cilantro for garnish*
- *red-pepper flakes for garnish*

Instructions

- Preheat the oven to 350 ° F.
- In a large ovenproof skillet, heat olive oil over medium heat. Add onion and sauté until tender, 4 to 5 minutes. Add the garlic and jalapeno pepper and sauté 1 more minute until fragrant.
- Add the kale and cook, 4 to 5 minutes, until completely tender if using fresh, or until heated through for 1 to 2 minutes when defrosting.
- Season with the cumin, cilantro, salt, pepper and cook for additional minute until it smells good.
- Pour the mixture into the bowl of a food processor or blender and blend until thickened. Add the broth and mash until thick and smooth.
- Clean the pan and grease it with non-stick cooking spray or add a baking paper. Return the spinach mixture to the pot and use a wooden spoon to make eight circular notches.
- Carefully break the eggs into the notches. Transfer the pot to the oven and cook until the egg whites are completely set but the yolks are still lightly stirred, 20 to 25 minutes.
- Sprinkle the shakshuka with parsley, cilantro and paprika flakes to taste. Eat immediately.

NUTRITION FACTS (PER SERVING)

Calories	280	
Total Fat	17.3g	22%
Saturated Fat	4.2g	21%
Cholesterol	372mg	124%
Sodium	287mg	12%
Total Carbohydrate	16.3g	6%
Dietary Fiber	2.5g	9%
Total Sugars	2.2g	
Protein	17.1g	

Tips: Leftovers will keep in the fridge for up to 1 week or can be frozen. To serve, warm in a pan with a little oil and top with the nuts / herbs.

SCRAMBLED EGGS

| Prep time: 5 min | Cook time: 5 min | Servings: 2 |

Ingredients

- *4 large eggs*
- *1/4 cup coconut milk*
- *salt, to taste*
- *freshly ground white pepper (or black pepper), to taste*
- *1-2 tbsp ghee*

Instructions

- Crack the eggs into a glass bowl and beat them until they turn light yellow.
- Add the milk to the eggs and season with salt and white pepper. Beat the eggs like crazy. If you're not up to it, you can use an electric mixer or a stand mixer with a whisk. Whichever device you use, try to get as much air as possible into the eggs.

66

- Preheat a solid-bottomed non-stick skillet over medium-low heat. Add the ghee and let it melt.
- When the saucepan is hot enough, pour the eggs into it. Do not stir. Let the eggs cook for up to a minute or until the bottom hardens but does not brown.
- Using a heat-resistant rubber spatula, gently press one the edge of the egg toward the center while tilting the pan to allow the egg, which is still liquid, to sink underneath. Repeat with the other edges until all of the liquid is gone.
- Turn off the heat and keep stirring the egg gently until all the raw parts are firm. Do not break the egg and keep the curd as big as possible. As you add more ingredients, add them quickly.
- Transfer to a plate when the eggs are ready, but still moist and soft. Serve immediately and enjoy.

NUTRITION FACTS (PER SERVING)

Calories	329	
Total Fat	30.7g	39%
Saturated Fat	21.2g	106%
Cholesterol	372mg	124%
Sodium	222mg	10%
Total Carbohydrate	2.5g	1%
Dietary Fiber	0.7g	2%
Total Sugars	1.8g	
Protein	13.3g	

Tips: Make it easy on yourself and cook your eggs in a nonstick sauté pan. Use a heat-resistant silicone spatula so it doesn't melt or scratch the pan.

2. MAIN MEAL RECIPES

ORANGE AND PORK STIR-FRY

Prep time: 20 min	Cook time: 15 min	Servings: 2

Ingredients

- *1.5 lbs. lean pork, thinly sliced*
- *2 oranges, peeled and cut into cubes*
- *1 bell pepper, diced*
- *3 garlic cloves*
- *2 tbsp coconut aminos*
- *3 green onions, sliced*
- *juice of 2 oranges*
- *zest of 1 orange*
- *1 tbsp avocado oil*
- *sea salt and freshly ground pepper*

Instructions

- In a small bowl, combine the orange zest, orange juice, chopped garlic and coconut amino acids and season to taste.
- Heat the avocado oil in a pan over medium-high heat.
- Brown meat on all sides, approx. 5 minutes. Remove and set aside.
- In the same pan, add the bell peppers and cook for 2 to 3 minutes.
- Pour the orange juice mixture into the pan and cook until the syrupy forms, 3 minutes.
- Add the oranges and chopped green onion and meat and mix everything thoroughly.
- Serve and enjoy!

NUTRITION FACTS (PER SERVING)		
Calories	292	
Total Fat	3.8g	5%
Saturated Fat	1g	5%
Cholesterol	47mg	16%
Sodium	255mg	11%
Total Carbohydrate	45.8g	17%
Dietary Fiber	6.8g	24%
Total Sugars	31.2g	
Protein	20.6g	

Tips: pork is particularly rich in thiamine — one of the B vitamins that plays an essential role in various bodily functions.

MUSHROOM LAMB STEW

Prep time: 5 min	Cook time: 25 min	Servings: 4

Ingredients

- *2 lbs. lamb cubes*
- *2 cups fresh mushrooms, sliced*
- *2 onions, sliced*
- *2 cups chicken stock*
- *2 garlic cloves, minced*
- *1 tbsp almond flour*
- *coconut oil*
- *sea salt and freshly ground black pepper*

Instructions

- Season the lamb cubes with sea salt and freshly ground black pepper.
- Heat the coconut oil in a casserole dish over medium heat and brown the cubes of meat on all sides.
- Add onion, garlic and mushrooms. Cook 4 to 5 minutes.
- Pour in the chicken stock and scrape the bottom of the pan, stirring well.
- Cover and simmer for 15 to 20 minutes.
- Adjust the spices and combine the starch with 2 tbsp. water, then mix with the stew. Stir well until the sauce thickens.

NUTRITION FACTS (PER SERVING)

Calories	380	
Total Fat	16.7g	21%
Saturated Fat	7.4g	37%
Cholesterol	147mg	49%
Sodium	608mg	26%
Total Carbohydrate	7.5g	3%
Dietary Fiber	1.8g	6%
Total Sugars	3.4g	
Protein	48.4 g	

Tips: Adding flour to stew is the most classic way to create its characteristic thick texture.

ASIAN TURKEY CABBAGE SALAD

Prep time: 20 min	Cook time: 15 min	Servings: 6

Ingredients

Turkey seasonings:

- *1 3/4 lbs. turkey breasts*
- *salt, garlic, onion, paprika powder*

Salad:

- *1 carrot (thinly sliced)*
- *8 cups Napa cabbage*
- *1 cup red cabbage, thinly sliced*
- *1/2 cup snow peas, roughly chopped*
- *some almond slices*

Aromatics:

- *1 large garlic clove, minced*
- *2 thin slices ginger, finely chopped*
- *2 bulbs scallions, chopped, separate white & green parts*
- *1/4 tsp red pepper flakes, optional*
- *1/8 tsp five spice powder*

Dressing:

- *1 tsp grated ginger*
- *2 tbsp toasted sesame oil*
- *2 tbsp apple cider vinegar*
- *2 tbsp coconut aminos*

Instructions

- Turkey: Season the turkey breast on both sides with salt, garlic, onions and paprika powder. Fry them in a pan with 1 tablespoon of ghee (or vegetable oil) until both sides are golden brown and cooked through. Cover lightly with foil and set aside.
- Fry the all aromatics with 1 tablespoon of vegetable oil. Season with a pinch of salt.
- Fry for 10 – 20 seconds.
- Add the cabbage and thinly sliced carrots. Gently stir them a few times until the vegetables are a little softer but still crispy. Season with salt. Let cool.
- Prepare the dressing. Mix all ingredients for dressing in a bowl.
- Combine the sautéed vegetables with thinly sliced red cabbage, chopped peas, sliced almonds and sliced turkey.
- Add in the dressings and shake it quickly and serve

NUTRITION FACTS (PER SERVING)

Calories	252	
Total Fat	7g	9%
Saturated Fat	1.1g	6%
Cholesterol	57mg	19%
Sodium	1434mg	62%
Total Carbohydrate	21.2g	8%
Dietary Fiber	5.7g	20%
Total Sugars	12.1g	
Protein	25.3g	

Tips: Cabbage is a very good source of dietary fiber, calcium, magnesium, and potassium.

CARROT SOUP

Prep time: 20 min	Cook time: 55 min	Servings: 6

Ingredients

- 4 tbsp avocado oil
- 1 onion, peeled and chopped
- salt and freshly ground black pepper
- 1-pound carrots, peeled and sliced
- 1 large sweet potato, peeled and diced
- wide strips of peel from ½ lime
- 2 bay leaves
- 6 cups vegetable stock or water

Instructions

- Heat the oil in a large, heavy-based saucepan over medium heat.
- Add the onion and cook, stirring occasionally, until tender but not golden, 8 to 10 minutes. Season with salt and pepper.
- Add the carrot, sweet potato, lime zest, bay leaves and 5 cups of vegetable broth. Cover the pot and cook, 30 to 45 minutes, until the vegetables are very tender.
- Discard the bay leaves. Reduce the soup in small amounts in a blender or food processor until very smooth. Add some of the remaining 1 cup of broth if the soup is too thick. Season with salt and pepper. Serve hot.

NUTRITION FACTS (PER SERVING)

Calories	88	
Total Fat	1.4g	2%
Saturated Fat	0.3g	1%
Cholesterol	0mg	0%
Sodium	141mg	6%
Total Carbohydrate	18.1g	7%
Dietary Fiber	4.5g	16%
Total Sugars	7.4g	
Protein	2.1g	

Tips: Freeze your soup to make it last and provide a quick last-minute meal. Simply double whatever recipe you are following. Cook all parts of the soup that need it, let it cool to room temperature, and then freeze!

BEEF WITH SPINACH, SWEET POTATOES AND MUSHROOMS

| Prep time: 20 min | Cook time: 40 min | Servings: 6 |

Ingredients

- *2 lb. beef sirloin, cubed*
- *2 sweet potatoes, peeled and diced*
- *10 mushrooms, sliced*
- *1 red onion, sliced*
- *2 garlic cloves, minced*
- *2 cups baby spinach*
- *1/2 cup beef stock*
- *1 cup coconut milk*
- *1 tbsp garlic powder*
- *1 tbsp onion powder*
- *1 tbsp paprika*
- *1 tbsp coconut oil*
- *sea salt and freshly ground black pepper*

Instructions

- Preheat the oven to 375 F.
- Combine garlic powder, onion powder and paprika in a bowl and season to taste.
- Season the beef pieces with the seasoning mix.
- Melt the coconut oil in a skillet over medium to high heat.
- Brown the beef in the skillet on both sides, 2 to 3 minutes per side; then put in a baking dish.
- Cook the diced sweet potatoes in a skillet over medium heat for 5 to 6 minutes. Add more coconut oil if needed.
- Add the onion, mushrooms and garlic to the sweet potatoes and cook for another 2 to 3 minutes.
- Place the sweet potatoes, onions, mushrooms and garlic in the baking dish.
- Pour in the coconut milk and the beef broth.
- Garnish with spinach leaves, mix everything.
- Place in the oven and cook, covered, for 18 to 20 minutes. Cook for another 10 minutes without the lid.

NUTRITION FACTS (PER SERVING)

Calories	480	
Total Fat	21.6g	28%
Saturated Fat	14g	70%
Cholesterol	134mg	45%
Sodium	186mg	8%
Total Carbohydrate	22.2g	8%
Dietary Fiber	4.5g	16%
Total Sugars	3.8g	
Protein	49.4g	

Tips: Cooked red meat is very healthy. It contains a lot of nutrients and healthy proteins, fats, vitamins, minerals. According to research, eating it could positively affect the function of your body as well as brain.

CHICKEN BREAST AND APPLE SKILLET

| Prep time: 20 min | Cook time: 15 min | Servings: 4 |

Ingredients

- *4 chicken breasts*
- *2 apples, cored and sliced*
- *1 tsp chili powder*
- *1 tsp ground cinnamon*
- *1/3 cup coconut milk*
- *1/2 – 1 cup apple butter*
- *coconut oil*
- *sea salt and freshly ground black pepper*

Instructions

- Season the chicken breast on both sides.
- Heat some coconut oil in a skillet over medium to high heat.

- Fry the chicken breast, 5 to 6 minutes per side, until cooked through. Remove and reserve.
- Add the apple slices and cook until tender, about 2 minutes.
- Pour in the apple butter, cinnamon, chili powder and coconut milk.
- Stir until well combined, then bring to a boil.
- Return the chicken breast to the pan and cook them hot.
- Serve the chicken breast with the apple slices.

NUTRITION FACTS (PER SERVING)

Calories	268	
Total Fat	11.3g	14%
Saturated Fat	7.2g	36%
Cholesterol	72mg	24%
Sodium	68mg	3%
Total Carbohydrate	18.3g	7%
Dietary Fiber	3.7g	13%
Total Sugars	13.1g	
Protein	24.6g	

Tips: Chicken is highly nutritious and a good source of protein. Adding chicken to your diet may help support weight loss, muscle growth, and bone health.

CAULIFLOWER AND SPINACH SOUP

Prep time: 20 min	Cook time: 15 min	Servings: 4

Ingredients

- *1 cauliflower, chopped*
- *1 bunch spinach, chopped*
- *2 celery, diced*
- *1 onion, diced*
- *1 tbsp fresh ginger (minced)*
- *3 garlic cloves (minced)*
- *1/2 tsp cumin powder*
- *1 1/2 tbsp curry powder*
- *1 tsp turmeric powder*

- *1/2 tsp paprika*
- *4 tbsp ghee*
- *2 cups vegetable stock*
- *1 cup coconut milk*
- *sea salt and freshly ground black pepper*

Instructions

- Melt the ghee in a saucepan over medium heat.
- Add onion, garlic and ginger. Cook for 2 to 3 minutes.
- Add the cauliflower and celery. Cook for 4 to 5 minutes, stirring occasionally.
- Sprinkle with spices: curry, turmeric, cumin, paprika, sea salt and black pepper. Stir everything.
- Pour in the vegetable stock and add the spinach.
- Cover and simmer 15 to 20 minutes until all the vegetables are tender.
- Mix the soup with a hand blender until the desired consistency is achieved.
- Pour in the coconut milk, mix quickly and cook until heated through. Adjust the seasonings and serve.

NUTRITION FACTS (PER SERVING)		
Calories	260	
Total Fat	21.9g	28%
Saturated Fat	18.3g	92%
Cholesterol	0mg	0%
Sodium	137mg	6%
Total Carbohydrate	15.8g	6%
Dietary Fiber	6.9g	24%
Total Sugars	5g	
Protein	5.8g	

Tips: Cook veggies such as onions, leeks or carrots on low-medium heat for a few minutes before adding any liquids. This will help blend the flavor better.

PULLED CHICKEN STUFFED SQUASH

Prep time: 20 min	Cook time: 8 hours	Servings: 6

Ingredients

- *4 lbs. chicken breast*
- *1 tbsp chili flakes*
- *1 tbsp ground sweet paprika*
- *1 tsp ground cumin*
- *1 tsp onion powder*
- *1 cup chicken stock*
- *2 spring onions, diced*
- *2 small spaghetti squashes, halved and seeded*
- *olive oil*
- *salt and black pepper*

Instructions

- Combine the chili flakes, paprika, cumin, onion and garlic powder in a bowl. Put in as much seasoning as desired.
- Rub the chicken breast with the herb mixture, making sure all sides are covered.
- Place the chicken breast with onion and chicken broth in the slow cooker. Cover and simmer for 6 to 8 hours.
- Take the chicken breast out of the slow cooker and chop it with forks. Remove the remaining juice from the slow cooker, return the pulled chicken. Cook for another 30 minutes over low heat.
- Preheat the oven to 400 F. Brush the squash flesh with olive oil and season to taste.
- Place the squash halves on a baking sheet (cut side up) and sauté for approx. 45 minutes.
- Remove the squash from the oven and fill with the pulled chicken. Garnish with fresh herbs if desired, and serve.

NUTRITION FACTS (PER SERVING)

Calories	392	
Total Fat	10.6g	14%
Saturated Fat	0.5g	2%
Cholesterol	194mg	65%
Sodium	305mg	13%
Total Carbohydrate	5.6g	2%
Dietary Fiber	1.8g	6%
Total Sugars	1.9g	
Protein	65.1g	

Tips: Yellow squash is also rich in manganese. This mineral helps to boost bone strength and helps the body's ability to process fats and carbohydrates.

SEAFOOD CHOWDER

Prep time: 20 min	Cook time: 30 min	Servings: 4

Ingredients

- *1 lb. salmon, roughly chopped*
- *10 shrimps, peeled and deveined*
- *1 cup crab meat, chopped*
- *1 onion, diced*
- *2 garlic cloves, minced*
- *1 daikon radish, peeled and chopped*
- *2 cups vegetable stock*
- *1 1/2 cups full-fat coconut milk*
- *2 tbsp coconut oil*
- *sea salt and freshly ground black pepper*

Instructions

- Heat the coconut oil in a large saucepan over medium heat.
- Add the shrimp to the pan and cook until pink, 2 to 3 minutes per side, set aside.
- Add the onion and garlic and cook, 3 to 4 minutes, stirring frequently.
- Place the chopped daikon in the pot and cook for 4 to 5 minutes.
- Add the salmon and cook for 2 to 3 minutes, add the vegetable stock and stir, scraping the bottom of the pan.
- Return the shrimp with the crab meat to the pot, cover and simmer for 12 to 15 minutes.
- Pour in the coconut milk and season to taste.

NUTRITION FACTS (PER SERVING)		
Calories	337	
Total Fat	24.3g	31%
Saturated Fat	17.5g	87%
Cholesterol	113mg	38%
Sodium	180mg	8%
Total Carbohydrate	6.6g	2%
Dietary Fiber	2.1g	7%
Total Sugars	3.2g	
Protein	25.5g	

Tips: Slip the whole fillets into simmering chowder. This will cook them gently but no worries, they'll break apart in when cooked.

TARRAGON-LEMON ROASTED TURKEY BREAST

Prep time: 10 min	Cook time: 25 min	Servings: 4

Ingredients

- *4 turkey breasts*
- *8 tarragon sprigs*
- *1 tbsp lemon zest*
- *3 garlic cloves, minced*
- *2 fennel bulbs, trimmed and sliced*
- *1 cup chicken stock*
- *avocado oil*
- *sea salt and freshly ground black pepper*

Instructions

- Preheat the oven to 350 F.
- Season the turkey breast with sea salt and freshly ground black pepper.

90

- Heat the avocado oil in an ovenproof skillet over medium heat.
- Fry the turkey breast 1 to 2 minutes per side and set aside.
- In the same casserole dish, add the tarragon, lemon zest, garlic and fennel. Cook for 2 to 3 minutes, stirring constantly.
- Return the turkey breast to the plate, pour in the chicken broth and simmer.
- Uncover in the preheated oven and bake for 15 to 20 minutes.

NUTRITION FACTS (PER SERVING)

Calories	201	
Total Fat	11.2g	14%
Saturated Fat	2.3g	11%
Cholesterol	18mg	6%
Sodium	694mg	30%
Total Carbohydrate	17.7g	6%
Dietary Fiber	7.6g	27%
Total Sugars	2g	
Protein	10.9g	

Tips: Tarragon may help decrease blood sugar by improving insulin sensitivity and the way your body metabolizes glucose.

TOMATO AND PORK SOUP

Prep time: 20 min	Cook time: 45 min	Servings: 4

Ingredients

- 1.5 lbs. pork meat, cut into cubes
- 3 cups diced tomatoes
- 3 red bell peppers, diced
- 2 carrots, diced
- 1 onion, diced
- 2 garlic cloves, minced
- 1/2 tbsp paprika
- 1/2 tbsp fresh rosemary, minced
- 6 cups chicken stock
- coconut oil
- sea salt and freshly ground black pepper

Instructions

- Heat the coconut oil in a large saucepan over medium heat.
- Season the pork cubes with sea salt and freshly ground black pepper.
- Roast the pork cubes for 1 to 2 minutes on each side.
- Add the carrots, garlic and onion and cook, 1 to 2 minutes, stirring frequently.
- Add all the remaining ingredients. Bring to a boil.
- Cover and simmer for 30 to 35 minutes.
- Adjust seasonings before serving and serve.

NUTRITION FACTS (PER SERVING)

Calories	352	
Total Fat	15.6g	20%
Saturated Fat	7.2g	36%
Cholesterol	100mg	33%
Sodium	1290mg	56%
Total Carbohydrate	19.9g	7%
Dietary Fiber	4.7g	17%
Total Sugars	11.9g	
Protein	33.1g	

Tips: Soups that are thick and heavy, can really benefit from a dash of dairy. Add some milk or sour cream to it.

SALMON WITH MANGOS

Prep time: 15 min	Cook time: 20 min	Servings: 4

Ingredients

- *4 Salmon fillets, skin removed*
- *2 mangos, sliced*
- *2 tomatoes, sliced*
- *1 onion, sliced*
- *Fresh cilantro*
- *2 tbsp avocado oil*
- *sea salt and freshly ground pepper*

Instructions

- Preheat the oven to 400 F.
- Place the mangoes, tomatoes and onions in the bottom of a baking dish.
- Place the trout on top, drizzle with olive oil and season to taste.
- Bake for 18 to 20 minutes or until desired doneness is reached.
- Sprinkle with fresh cilantro and serve.

NUTRITION FACTS (PER SERVING)

Calories	369	
Total Fat	12.7g	16%
Saturated Fat	1.9g	10%
Cholesterol	78mg	26%
Sodium	87mg	4%
Total Carbohydrate	30.7g	11%
Dietary Fiber	4.5g	16%
Total Sugars	25.8g	
Protein	37g	

Tips: Canned wild salmon is an excellent source of both vitamin D and calcium – two essential bone-building nutrients.

BEEF AND VEGETABLE SOUP

Prep time: 15 min	Cook time: 20 min	Servings: 4

Ingredients

- *4 cups roast beef, shredded*
- *1 onion, chopped*
- *4 carrots, sliced*
- *1 sweet potato diced*
- *4 cups beef stock*
- *1/4 cup coconut milk*
- *2 garlic cloves, minced*
- *2 tbsp fresh chives, minced*
- *2 tbsp coconut oil*
- *sea salt and freshly ground black pepper*

Instructions

- In a large saucepan, heat the coconut oil over medium-high heat.
- Add the garlic and onion and cook, 2 to 3 minutes, until tender.
- Add the carrots and sweet potato to the pot and cook for another 2 to 3 minutes.
- Pour in the beef broth and bring to a boil.
- Bring to a boil and simmer for 15 to 20 minutes or until the vegetables are tender.
- Add the beef and cook until lukewarm.
- Add the coconut milk and season to taste.
- Serve the soup with fresh chives.

NUTRITION FACTS (PER SERVING)		
Calories	232	
Total Fat	8.2g	11%
Saturated Fat	4.9g	25%
Cholesterol	61mg	20%
Sodium	717mg	31%
Total Carbohydrate	14.9g	5%
Dietary Fiber	3g	11%
Total Sugars	5.3g	
Protein	24.3g	

Tips: lean beef is rich in various vitamins and minerals, especially iron and zinc.

TUNA WITH VEGGIES IN TERIYAKI-STYLE

Prep time: 15 min	Cook time: 20 min	Servings: 4

Ingredients

- *2 tuna fillets, skinless and cut into large chunks*
- *2 cups broccoli, cut into florets*
- *2 carrots, sliced*
- *1 red onion, thinly sliced*
- *2 cups bean sprouts*
- *2 garlic cloves, minced*
- *1 thumb-sized fresh ginger, minced*
- *1/4 cup coconut aminos*
- *1 tbsp raw honey*
- *1/2 tsp red pepper flakes*
- *2 tbsp coconut oil*
- *sea salt and freshly ground black pepper*

Instructions

- Season the tuna with sea salt and freshly ground black pepper.
- In a small bowl, combine the coconut amino acids, raw honey and paprika flakes.
- Heat the coconut oil in a skillet over medium to high heat.
- Cook the tuna pieces in the pan for 3 to 4 minutes per side, then remove them from the pan.
- Add the onion, ginger and garlic and cook, stirring constantly, 2 to 3 minutes. Add broccoli and carrots. Cook another 4 to 5 minutes or until tender.
- Pour in the coconut amino sauce and mix everything together.
- Return the tuna to the pan, add the bean sprouts and mix everything gently. Serve warm.

NUTRITION FACTS (PER SERVING)

Calories	340	
Total Fat	23g	29%
Saturated Fat	6g	30%
Cholesterol	0mg	0%
Sodium	60mg	3%
Total Carbohydrate	20.4g	7%
Dietary Fiber	2.6g	9%
Total Sugars	7.8g	
Protein	16.3g	

Tips: Adding cold meat will instantly cool off your wok. To avoid this, let the meat sit out at room temperature for 20 minutes before you cook it.

TROUT, AVOCADO AND EGG SALAD

Prep time: 20 min	Cook time: 0 min	Servings: 4

Ingredients

- *2 cups flaked trout, cooked*
- *2 hard-boiled eggs, diced*
- *1 bell pepper, diced*
- *1 avocado, diced*
- *1/2 red onion, minced*
- *1/4 cup homemade mayonnaise*
- *1/4 tsp Cayenne Pepper*
- *juice from half lemon*
- *1/4 cup fresh parsley, minced*
- *2 tbsp avocado oil*
- *sea salt and freshly ground black pepper*

Instructions

- In a bowl, whisk together the mayonnaise, parsley, lemon juice, cayenne pepper and avocado oil until well mixed.
- In a salad bowl, add the trout, cubed eggs, bell pepper, avocado and red onion.
- Pour the mayonnaise mixture over the trout mixture.
- Mix everything gently until everything is well combined.
- Refrigerate until ready to eat and serve with fresh or garnished vegetables as is.

NUTRITION FACTS (PER SERVING)

Calories	343	
Total Fat	27.2g	35%
Saturated Fat	5.4g	27%
Cholesterol	115mg	38%
Sodium	162mg	7%
Total Carbohydrate	12.1g	4%
Dietary Fiber	4.3g	15%
Total Sugars	3.7g	
Protein	14.8g	

Tips: Put the pot over high heat and bring to a boil. Once the water is at a rolling boil, turn off the heat and cover the pot with the lid. Allow the eggs to sit in the hot water for the following times according to the desired doneness: 3 minutes for SOFT boiled; 6 minutes for MEDIUM boiled; 12 minutes for HARD boiled.

TURKEY SALAD WITH BALSAMIC

| Prep time: 20 min | Cook time: 0 min | Servings: 4 |

Ingredients

- 2 turkey breasts
- 8 cups mixed greens
- 1 bell pepper, diced
- 1 cup grape tomatoes, halved
- 1/2 red onion, sliced
- 1 avocado, sliced
- 1/2 tsp oregano
- 1/2 tbsp dried onion flakes
- 1/2 tbsp garlic powder
- 1/2 tbsp paprika
- olive oil
- sea salt and freshly ground black pepper

Balsamic Dressing

- 1/2 cup olive oil
- 1/4 cup balsamic vinegar
- 1 tbsp fresh lemon juice
- 2 tbsp apple cider vinegar
- 2 tbsp fresh parsley, minced
- 2 tsp fresh basil, minced
- 1 tsp dried oregano
- 1 garlic clove, minced
- sea salt and freshly ground black pepper

Instructions

- Season the turkey with the oregano, onion flakes, garlic, paprika, sea salt and black pepper.
- Heat the olive oil over medium to high heat.
- Fry the turkey breast in the pan. And cook until no longer pink, 6 to 8 minutes per side, and let stand 4 to 5 minutes.
- Cut the turkey breast into slices and set aside.
- Combine all the ingredients for the balsamic dressing in a bowl and mixed well.
- Combine mixed salads, peppers, grape tomatoes, red onions and avocado in a salad bowl.
- Top with turkey breast and drizzle dressing over salad.
- Give everything a light touch and serve.

NUTRITION FACTS (PER SERVING)

Calories	405	
Total Fat	12.6g	16%
Saturated Fat	3.7g	19%
Cholesterol	9mg	3%
Sodium	353mg	15%
Total Carbohydrate	59.6g	22%
Dietary Fiber	21g	75%
Total Sugars	16.1g	
Protein	16.1g	

Tips: Set the timer and cook the turkey about 3 to 4 minutes per pound. Cook all dark meat to an internal temperature of 175° F to 180° F, and all white meat to an internal temperature of 165° F to 170° F.

CHICKEN, KALE, AND BROCCOLI SOUP

| Prep time: 25 min | Cook time: 45 min | Servings: 4 |

Ingredients

- *1 lb. ground chicken*
- *4 onions, chopped*
- *3 carrots, sliced*
- *1 bell pepper, cut into pieces*
- *15 oz can dice tomato*
- *5 cups chicken stock*
- *1 1/2 cup broccoli, minced*
- *4 cups kale, chopped leaves, ribs discarded,*
- *2 tbsp ghee*
- *salt and pepper to taste*

Instructions

- Heat the ghee in a saucepan over medium-high heat.
- Add the onion, carrots, broccoli and bell peppers.
- Cook for 10 minutes, stirring frequently (until veggies are soft and ready).
- Add the chicken vegetables and cook until the meat is cooked through 6 to 8 minutes.
- Add the chicken stock, tomatoes, season with salt and pepper and bring to a boil.
- Add the kale, reduce the heat to low and simmer for 15 minutes, with the lid on. If desired, sprinkle with fresh herbs or pepper before serving.

NUTRITION FACTS (PER SERVING)

Calories	389	
Total Fat	16.1g	21%
Saturated Fat	8.4g	42%
Cholesterol	101mg	34%
Sodium	1352mg	59%
Total Carbohydrate	24g	9%
Dietary Fiber	5.2g	19%
Total Sugars	8.8g	
Protein	38.5g	

Tips: Homemade chicken Stock: You simply add your chicken to the pot, along with water, aromatic vegetables (i.e., carrots, celery, and onions), and a few seasonings, like whole black peppercorns and a bay leaf. Then, turn it on to the "bone broth" setting and walk away. When the timer goes off, release the steam, strain, and either chill for later or proceed to make your soup.

SALMON WITH TOASTED GARLIC BROCCOLI

| Prep time: 40 min | Cook time: 25 min | Servings: 4 |

Ingredients

- *4 salmon fillets, skin on*
- *3 tbsp avocado oil*
- *6 garlic cloves, minced*
- *2 tbsp lemon juice*
- *1/2 tsp dried basil*
- *1 tbsp fresh parsley, finely chopped*
- *1 lemon, wedged*
- *1 lb. broccoli, cut into florets*
- *2 tbsp coconut oil*
- *sea salt and freshly ground black pepper*

Instructions

- Grease a large baking sheet and place the skin on the salmon fillets, making sure they do not overlap. Season with salt and pepper.
- Heat the oil in a small saucepan over medium heat and mix with the chopped garlic, lemon juice, basil and parsley. Simmer for 2 minutes. Pour the mixture over the fillets and let them marinate for at least 30 minutes.
- Turn the grill on high and grill the halibut for about 10 minutes, or until the fish is white and flaky. Serve with lemon wedges.
- For the broccoli: bring a pot of water to a boil. Place the broccoli in the pot and cook until tender, about 5 minutes.
- Put coconut oil in a large skillet over medium heat. Fry the chopped garlic in oil. Stir frequently and let the garlic brown for about 3 minutes. Remove the garlic and set aside for later use.
- Transfer the cooked broccoli to the pot you used earlier. If desired, add more olive oil and fry for about 3 minutes. Add the roasted garlic and season with salt and pepper.

NUTRITION FACTS (PER SERVING)

Calories	339	
Total Fat	15.7g	20%
Saturated Fat	8.5g	43%
Cholesterol	78mg	26%
Sodium	131mg	6%
Total Carbohydrate	6.6g	2%
Dietary Fiber	2.3g	8%
Total Sugars	1.7g	
Protein	42.7 g	

Tips: Blanching broccoli is not necessary for stir frying, especially if you cut the florets small. If the florets are big, they may take longer to cook in the wok,

LEMON-ROSEMARY SEARED TROUT

| Prep time: 15 min | Cook time: 10 min | Servings: 4 |

Ingredients

- *4 trout fillets, skinless*
- *2 garlic cloves, minced*
- *2 tsp fresh rosemary, minced*
- *1 cup fresh lemon juice*
- *2 tbsp fresh orange juice*
- *1/2 cup chicken stock*
- *2 tsp lemon zest*
- *1 tbsp tapioca starch (optional)*
- *coconut oil*
- *sea salt and freshly ground black pepper*

Instructions

- Season the trout fillets on both sides.
- Heat coconut oil in a skillet over medium to high heat.
- Cook the trout fillets in the pan for 4 to 5 minutes per side and set aside.
- In a bowl, combine the orange juice, lemon juice, chicken broth and lemon zest.
- In the same pan, cook the garlic and rosemary for 1 to 2 minutes.
- Pour the lemon juice mixture into the pot and bring it to a boil.
- Reduce the heat to medium-low and season to taste. If you like a thicker sauce, mix 1 tbsp tapioca starch with 1 tbsp of cold water and add to the pot.
- Return the trout to the pan. Pour the sauce over the trout fillets and serve.

NUTRITION FACTS (PER SERVING)

Calories	180	
Total Fat	9.3g	12%
Saturated Fat	4.4g	22%
Cholesterol	46mg	15%
Sodium	150mg	7%
Total Carbohydrate	5.4g	2%
Dietary Fiber	0.6g	2%
Total Sugars	2.2g	
Protein	17.3g	

Tips: The best time of day to catch trout is early morning from dawn until 2 hours after sunrise and the second-best time of the day is late afternoon from 3 hours prior to sunset until dusk.

BAKED MUSTARD CHICKEN

Prep time: 15 min	Cook time: 10 min	Servings: 4

Ingredients

- *4 chicken breasts, skinless and boneless*
- *1/4 cup Dijon mustard*
- *3 tbsp whole grain mustard*
- *3 tbsp maple syrup*
- *4 tbsp chicken stock*
- *2 tbsp coconut oil*
- *4 sprigs fresh rosemary*
- *sea salt and freshly ground black pepper*

Instructions

- Preheat the oven to 400 degrees F.
- Combine Dijon mustard, whole mustard, maple syrup and chicken broth in a bowl.
- Heat coconut oil in a skillet over medium to high heat.
- Season the chicken breast to taste and brown in the preheated skillet for 2 to 3 minutes per side.
- Cover the golden chicken breast with the mustard sauce and cover well.
- Transfer to a baking dish, cover each breast with a sprig of fresh rosemary and bake for 25 to 30 minutes.

NUTRITION FACTS (PER SERVING)

Calories	398	
Total Fat	18.9g	24%
Saturated Fat	9g	45%
Cholesterol	130mg	43%
Sodium	403mg	18%
Total Carbohydrate	12.5g	5%
Dietary Fiber	1g	4%
Total Sugars	9.1g	
Protein	43g	

Tips: Cooking a boneless and skinless chicken breast in a hot cast iron pan is by far the easiest and tastiest way to cook the breast.

HONEY GARLIC TURKEY AND VEGETABLES

Prep time: 20 min	Cook time: 40 min	Servings: 2

Ingredients

- *2 turkey breasts, boneless, skinless*
- *1/2 head cauliflower, diced*
- *1/4 cup cherry tomatoes, halved*
- *1/2 zucchini, sliced*
- *1 sweet potatoes, diced*
- *1/4 tsp oregano (dried)*
- *1/4 tsp basil (dried)*
- *1 tbsp coconut oil*
- *1 tbsp ghee*
- *1 tbsp raw honey*

- *1/2 tbsp mustard*
- *2 garlic cloves*
- *fresh parsley (for garnishing)*
- *salt and black pepper*

Instructions

- Preheat the oven to 400 F.
- Combine coconut oil, ghee, honey, mustard, garlic (minced or chopped), oregano and basil in a bowl. Season to taste.
- Place the turkey in a saucepan and put the sweet potatoes and other vegetables around the turkey.
- Pour the mixture of coconut oil and herbs over all the ingredients and mix.
- Place in the oven and bake for 25 to 30 minutes, until the turkey is cooked through and the vegetables are tender.
- Serve with fresh parsley (or other fresh herbs you like).

NUTRITION FACTS (PER SERVING)

Calories	316	
Total Fat	14.4g	19%
Saturated Fat	10.1g	50%
Cholesterol	35mg	12%
Sodium	516mg	22%
Total Carbohydrate	38.6g	14%
Dietary Fiber	6.1g	22%
Total Sugars	13.6g	
Protein	11g	

Tips: Just make sure you uncover the lid about 30 minutes before the turkey's done roasting so the outer part has a chance to get crispy.

GROUND PORK AND ZUCCHINI STIR-FRY

Prep time: 20 min	Cook time: 20 min	Servings: 4

Ingredients

- 1 lb. ground pork
- 1 large zucchini,
- 1 onion, diced
- 2 bell peppers, thinly sliced
- 1 head broccoli florets
- 1 green onion, thinly sliced
- 1/4 cup coconut aminos
- 2 tbsp apple cider vinegar
- 2 tbsp maple syrup
- 2 garlic cloves, minced
- 1 tbsp. fresh ginger, minced

Instructions

- Combine the coconut amino, apple cider vinegar, maple syrup, garlic and ginger for the sauce in the pan in a bowl.
- Fry the pork and onion in a pan over medium heat.
- Add the peppers and broccoli florets and cook, 6 to 8 minutes, until the vegetables are tender.
- Pour the sauce, add the zucchini and mix everything until well coated.
- Cook another 2 to 3 minutes, adjust the spices and garnish with green onions.

NUTRITION FACTS (PER SERVING)

Calories	264	
Total Fat	4.5g	6%
Saturated Fat	1.4g	7%
Cholesterol	83mg	28%
Sodium	102mg	4%
Total Carbohydrate	22.8g	8%
Dietary Fiber	3.2g	11%
Total Sugars	12.1g	
Protein	32.5g	

Tips: Zucchini is packed with many important vitamins, minerals, and antioxidants. It has a high fiber content and a low-calorie count. Fiber plays an important role in digestion and may limit the likelihood of suffering from a variety of GI issues.

SAUTÉED TURKEY AND CABBAGE

Prep time: 20 min	Cook time: 20 min	Servings: 4

Ingredients

- *2 turkey breasts, skinless, boneless and sliced*
- *1 head of cabbage, shredded*
- *2 carrots, shredded*
- *3 tbsp paprika*
- *3 tomatoes, pureed*
- *1 cup chicken stock*
- *2 tbsp coconut oil*
- *sea salt and freshly ground black pepper*

Instructions

- Melt the coconut oil in a skillet over medium to high heat.

- Cook the turkey slices until golden brown on each side.
- When you are almost done, add the shredded cabbage and carrots to the pan and cook, stirring, for 4-5 minutes.
- Add the tomatoes, chicken broth, paprika and season to taste.
- Stir everything well and bring to a boil.
- Lower the heat and simmer for 10 to 12 minutes to make sure the turkey is cooked through.
- Remove from the heat and serve hot.

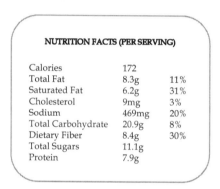

NUTRITION FACTS (PER SERVING)

Calories	172	
Total Fat	8.3g	11%
Saturated Fat	6.2g	31%
Cholesterol	9mg	3%
Sodium	469mg	20%
Total Carbohydrate	20.9g	8%
Dietary Fiber	8.4g	30%
Total Sugars	11.1g	
Protein	7.9g	

Tips: Cabbage is a nutritious vegetable that has many applications and goes well with everything from pork and beef to lamb, chicken, turkey and other poultry.

BEEF STUFFED BELL PEPPERS

| Prep time: 20 min | Cook time: 45 min | Servings: 4 |

Ingredients

- 4 bell peppers (green, red, yellow or orange)
- 3 tbsp coconut oil
- 1 onion minced
- 1 clove garlic minced
- 1 red bell pepper minced
- 1 lb. ground beef
- 10 oz cherry tomatoes
- 1 oz raisins
- zest from one lemon
- 1 tbsp fresh oregano, minced
- 1 tbsp fresh cilantro, minced
- 1 tbsp fresh marjoram, minced
- sea salt and freshly ground black pepper to taste

Instructions

- Preheat your oven to 350F.
- Halve 4 bell peppers. Remove the seeds and the white membrane.
- Place the peppers in a baking dish and apply 1 tablespoon of coconut oil to all the peppers. Make sure they are all covered when you do this.
- Put the peppers in the oven for 20 minutes.
- Melt 2 tbsp of coconut oil in a pan, over medium-high heat.
- Add the garlic, onion and chopped red bell pepper for 2 minutes or cook until tender. As soon as the vegetables are tender, add the beef and season with salt and pepper.
- When the meat is almost done, add the cherry tomatoes, raisins, lemon zest and fresh herbs and cook for a few more minutes.
- Fill all the precooked peppers with the beef mixture.
- Cover the peppers with foil and bake for 25 minutes.
- Remove the foil and bake again for 5 to 10 minutes.

NUTRITION FACTS (PER SERVING)

Calories	387	
Total Fat	17.9g	23%
Saturated Fat	11.5g	58%
Cholesterol	101mg	34%
Sodium	93mg	4%
Total Carbohydrate	22g	8%
Dietary Fiber	4.6g	17%
Total Sugars	13.3g	
Protein	37.1g	

Tips: Unless you're in a rush, it's best to cook your stuffed peppers before freezing. This will save you a lot of time later on when it's time to bake them. If you're just eating one or two peppers at a time, then wrap them individually before freezing.

CHICKEN STEW

| Prep time: 30 min | Cook time: 120 min | Servings: 4 |

Ingredients

- *8 chicken thighs about 1 1/2 pounds, diced*
- *2 tbsp coconut oil*
- *2 carrots diced*
- *1 small onion*
- *2 stalks celery diced*
- *5 tbsp almond flour divided*
- *1/2 tsp rosemary*
- *1/2 tsp thyme*
- *1/4 tsp sage*
- *salt and pepper to taste*
- *1 1/2 cups sweet potatoes peeled and diced*
- *1/2 red pepper finely diced*
- *4 cups chicken broth*
- *1 cup green beans or peas*
- *1/2 cup coconut cream*

Instructions

- In a large saucepan or casserole, brown the chicken in 1 tablespoon of coconut oil. Take out of the pot and keep.
- Cook the onion, carrot and celery in the remaining coconut oil for about 3 minutes or until the onion is slightly tender. Add 3 tablespoons of almond flour, spices and salt and pepper to taste. Cook over medium heat for about 2 minutes.
- Add the sweet potatoes, red peppers, golden chicken and broth. Bring to a boil, reduce heat and simmer, covered, for 30 minutes.
- Remove the lid and add the green beans and coconut cream. Thicken if desired and simmer, uncovered, for an additional 10 minutes.
- To thicken: combine the remaining 2 tablespoons of almond flour and 1 cup of water or broth in a glass. Shake very well and gradually add to the boiling stew to achieve the desired consistency.

NUTRITION FACTS (PER SERVING)

Calories	487	
Total Fat	9.8g	13%
Saturated Fat	4.6g	23%
Cholesterol	50mg	17%
Sodium	454mg	20%
Total Carbohydrate	90.3g	33%
Dietary Fiber	10.5g	38%
Total Sugars	70.1g	
Protein	18.1g	

Tips: Add in some fresh herbs before serving. Fresh herbs should be added at the end of the cooking time, as they lose their flavor as they simmer. Use dried herbs for cooking.

3. DINNER RECIPES

CRISPY SWEET POTATO LATKES

Prep time: 10 min	Cook time: 15 min	Servings: 22 pices

Ingredients

- *2 pounds sweet potatoes peeled*
- *1 large onion peeled and quartered*
- *2 large eggs*
- *1 1/2 tbsp almond flour*
- *1 tsp fine sea salt*
- *1/2 tsp freshly ground black pepper*
- *1/2-3/4 cup coconut oil, for frying*
- *Scallions or chives thinly sliced, for garnish*

Instructions

- Preheat your oven to 300 ° F and line a large baking sheet with parchment paper. You're not going to cook the latkes, it's just to keep them warm and crisp before serving.

126

- Mash the sweet potatoes and onions with a food processor using a paper shredder or hand grater. If you are using a food processor, you may need to cut the sweet potatoes to fit them properly.
- Line a large bowl with a few layers of paper towels and add the crumbled mixture to the bowl. Squeeze as much water as possible out of the sink. You can do this twice with clean paper towels to remove as much water as possible. After squeezing, remove the paper towels and pour the mixture into a large mixing bowl.
- Add the eggs, almond flour, salt and pepper. Mix with your hands until everything is well combined.
- Heat the oil in a large skillet over medium heat. You will need to set the heat to medium / medium high as you work to keep the oil at the right temperature. Cover a large plate with paper towels to drain each batch.
- Drop 1-1 / 2-2 round tablespoons of the mixture into the pot and gently crush and squeeze to smooth. It is important not to fill the pan to keep the oil hot.
- Fry until golden brown on one side for about 1-3 minutes (look at them), then gently flip with a spatula. Continue cooking until the second side is golden and crisp, another 1 to 3 minutes. Place on paper towels and drain briefly, then onto the prepared baking sheet. Place in the oven to keep warm while roasting additional batches.
- Repeat with the remaining mixture until used; Depending on the size, you get between 22 and 26. Serve immediately with chives or spring onions, applesauce or ranch (or keep warm in the oven).

NUTRITION FACTS (PER SERVING)

Calories	61	
Total Fat	5.2g	7%
Saturated Fat	4.1g	20%
Cholesterol	16mg	5%
Sodium	88mg	4%
Total Carbohydrate	3.5g	1%
Dietary Fiber	0.5g	2%
Total Sugars	0.9g	
Protein	0.9 g	

Tips: Sweet potatoes are a great source of fiber, vitamins, and minerals.

BAKED BLOOMING ONION

Prep time: 15 min	Cook time: 35 min	Servings: 4

Ingredients

- 5 small Onions
- 1 Egg
- 1/2 cup Blanched almond flour
- 1/2 cup coconut flour
- 1 tbsp paprika
- 1/2 tsp sea salt
- 1/4 tsp Cayenne pepper
- 2 tbsp avocado oil

Instructions

- First, cut off half an inch from the pointed side of the onion and peel it. Place the chopped onion side down. Starting half an inch from the top, cut the onion in half, making 4 cuts all around. Repeat between cuts until you have between 8 and 12 cuts. Turn the onion over and gently shake the petals.

- Preheat the oven to 400 ° F and line a baking sheet with parchment paper or aluminum foil. Beat an egg in a small bowl, mix the flour and spices in another bowl. Dip an onion in the egg, making sure all the petals are covered inside and out. Drain off the excess and gently add the flour mixture.

- Cover the onions with foil and bake for 7 minutes, remove the foil and bake for another 8 minutes. Using a spray brush, lightly brush the onions with a little melted coconut oil. Return to oven for another 15 minutes. Check the color and see if they are crisp. Otherwise, fry them over high heat for 5 minutes

NUTRITION FACTS (PER SERVING)

Calories	126	
Total Fat	7.4g	9%
Saturated Fat	1.1g	5%
Cholesterol	33mg	11%
Sodium	210mg	9%
Total Carbohydrate	10.9g	4%
Dietary Fiber	4g	14%
Total Sugars	3.3g	
Protein	4.8g	

Tips: You can reheat a blooming onion by placing it in the oven at 350 degrees F and baking for 10-15 minutes.

131

ROASTED SPICED CAULIFLOWER

Prep time: 5 min	Cook time: 35 min	Servings: 6

Ingredients

- *1 tbsp of coconut oil*
- *1 head of cauliflower, trimmed at the base, with green leaves removed*
- *1 can almond milk*
- *juice of 1 lemon*
- *zest of 1 lemon*
- *2 tbsp of chili powder*
- *1 tbsp of cumin*
- *1 tbsp of garlic minced*
- *1 tsp of curry powder*
- *2 tsp of sea salt*
- *1 tsp of black pepper*

Instructions

- Preheat your oven to 400 degrees. Take the coconut oil and place it in a baking dish. Throw it in the oven to melt it.
- Combine the almond milk, lemon zest, lemon juice, chili powder, cumin, garlic powder and curry powder in a bowl. Season with salt and pepper.
- Now take your cauliflower by the head and dip it into the bowl. Brush everything with the marinade. Use your hands to make sure it is well covered all over.
- Place the cauliflower in the baking dish you used to melt the coconut oil. Roast for 30 to 40 minutes until dry and lightly browned. A crust will form on the surface of the cauliflower in the marinade.
- Let it cool for a few minutes before cutting it into pieces and serving!

NUTRITION FACTS (PER SERVING)

Calories	135	
Total Fat	12.2g	16%
Saturated Fat	10.5g	52%
Cholesterol	0mg	0%
Sodium	722mg	31%
Total Carbohydrate	7.1g	3%
Dietary Fiber	2.6g	9%
Total Sugars	2.7g	
Protein	2.3g	

Tips: Of the 100 grams of cauliflower in one serving, 92 grams are water. That means this veggie can help keep you hydrated. It's also a good source of fiber.

FRIED ZUCCHINI WITH COOL MINT DIP

| Prep time: 15 min | Cook time: 30 min | Servings: 12 pieces |

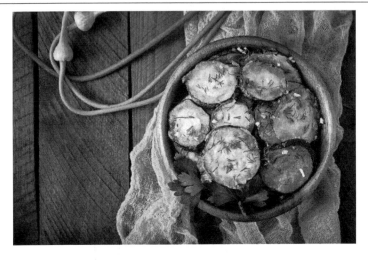

Ingredients

Fried zucchini ingredients

- *2 zucchinis; thicker ones are better*
- *3 tbsp almond flour*
- *1 tsp paprika*
- *2 tbsp coconut milk*
- *1 egg*
- *sea salt to taste*
- *coconut oil for frying*

Cool mint dip ingredients

- *1/2 cup coconut milk*
- *2 tsp lemon juice*
- *1 tbsp dried parsley*
- *1 tsp dried mint*
- *1/4 tsp garlic powder*
- *1/8 tsp salt*
- *1 pinch ground black pepper*

Instructions

Cool mint dip ingredients

- Combine all the ingredients for the sauce in a blender.
- If it is too thick, add coconut water to the coconut milk.
- Store in the refrigerator until ready to serve.

Fried zucchini

- Whisk the egg and coconut milk in a small bowl. Put aside.
- Place the almond flour and paprika in a large zippered plastic bag. Shake and save to mix.
- Heat a layer of coconut oil in a heavy skillet over medium-medium heat to about 1 cm deep.
- Cut the zucchini into 1/4-inch round slices.
- Add the zucchini slices to a plastic bag and shake to coat them with the dry mixture.
- Remove the slices from the bag and pat them lightly to remove loose spices.
- Then dip each slice in the mixture of egg and almond milk.
- Carefully place the seasoned zucchini slices in the hot coconut oil.
- Cook for about a minute on each side or until golden brown.

- Remove from the pan and place on a plate with paper towels to soak up any excess oil.
- Sprinkle with sea salt to taste.
- Serve with mint dip and enjoy!

NUTRITION FACTS (PER SERVING)

Calories	137	
Total Fat	9.5g	12%
Saturated Fat	7.7g	38%
Cholesterol	41mg	14%
Sodium	183mg	8%
Total Carbohydrate	9.6g	4%
Dietary Fiber	4.9g	18%
Total Sugars	2.3g	
Protein	4.2g	

Tips: You can use paper towels to press out excess liquid of Zucchini, prior to coating them.

SAUTÉED SPINACH WITH STUFFED MUSHROOMS

| Prep time: 5 min | Cook time: 35 min | Servings: 6 |

Ingredients

- *5 mushrooms*
- *2 spring onions*
- *1 lb. ground chicken*
- *1/8 tsp turmeric*
- *1/2 tsp garlic powder*
- *handful of spinach*
- *sea salt*
- *1-2 tbsp avocado oil*

Instructions

- First, remove the stems from the mushrooms and cut them finely.
- Then chop the spring onions.
- Fry over medium heat and add 1/2 tbsp avocado oil. Brown the mushrooms, garlic powder and spring onions. Add the turmeric. Once the onions are tender, about a minute or two, add the ground chicken. Cook the meat well. Add the spinach last until it wilts.
- Fill the mushroom caps with the ground chicken mixture and bake at 250F for 5 minutes.
- Serve and enjoy.

NUTRITION FACTS (PER SERVING)

Calories	65	
Total Fat	2.5g	3%
Saturated Fat	0.7g	3%
Cholesterol	25mg	8%
Sodium	125mg	5%
Total Carbohydrate	1.7g	1%
Dietary Fiber	0.6g	2%
Total Sugars	0.6g	
Protein	9g	

Tips: Mushrooms are a rich, low calorie source of fiber, protein, and antioxidants. They may also mitigate the risk of developing serious health conditions, such as Alzheimer's, heart disease, cancer, and diabetes.

HEALTHY CARROT FRIES

Prep time: 5 min	Cook time: 35 min	Servings: 4

Ingredients

- *8 large carrots*
- *1 tbsp coconut oil*
- *1 tsp garlic powder*
- *salt and pepper, to taste*
- *optional topping: fresh cilantro*

Almond Dipping Sauce

- *1/2 cup raw almond, soaked*
- *1 1/2 tbsp red curry paste*
- *1 tbsp coconut aminos*
- *2 tbsp lime juice*
- *1/2 tsp garlic powder*

- *1/2 tsp red pepper flakes*
- *1/2 tsp ginger*
- *1/4 cup water*

Instructions

- Soak the almonds the night before. Put them in a small bowl and cover with water. If you forgot to soak them, add them to hot water while the carrots are cooking.
- Preheat the oven to 375 degrees F. Cut the carrots into matchsticks. Transfer to a large bowl and toss with coconut oil, garlic powder, salt and pepper. Place on two baking sheets lined with parchment paper and distribute evenly. Make sure they aren't too close together.
- Bake for 20 minutes, stir / flip and bake another 15 minutes.
- While the fried carrots are cooking, prepare the sauce. Put all the ingredients in a blender and stir until smooth.
- As soon as the carrots are ready, sprinkle with fresh cilantro.

NUTRITION FACTS (PER SERVING)

Calories	171	
Total Fat	9.4g	12%
Saturated Fat	3.4g	17%
Cholesterol	0mg	0%
Sodium	106mg	5%
Total Carbohydrate	20.4g	7%
Dietary Fiber	5.3g	19%
Total Sugars	8.1g	
Protein	3.9g	

Tips: Carrots are a good source of antioxidants, fiber and vitamin K1.

CABBAGE CHIPS

Prep time: 10 min	Cook time: 2 hours	Servings: 6

Ingredients

- *1 head of cabbage, red or green (savoy works well)*
- *coconut oil*
- *sea salt*

Instructions

- Preheat the oven to 200 ° F / 93 ° C.
- Cut the cabbage in half and cut the core. Separate the cabbage leaves. Cut large leaves into halves or quarters.
- Place cabbage leaves on wire racks on baking sheets.
- Bake until crisp. Smaller (thinner) sheets will take about 2 hours, larger (thicker) sheets may take up to 3 hours.
- When the leaves are cooked, brush with coconut oil and sprinkle with sea salt and dill.

NUTRITION FACTS (PER SERVING)

Calories	72	
Total Fat	2.5g	3%
Saturated Fat	2g	10%
Cholesterol	0mg	0%
Sodium	115mg	5%
Total Carbohydrate	12.1g	4%
Dietary Fiber	5.2g	19%
Total Sugars	6.7g	
Protein	2.7g	

Tips: Many studies have suggested that increasing consumption of plant-based foods like cabbage decreases the risk of diabetes, obesity, heart disease, and overall mortality. It can also help promote a healthy complexion, increased energy, and an overall lower weight.

SWEET AND SPICY MEAT BALLS

| Prep time: 15 min | Cook time: 30 min | Servings: 45 pieces |

Ingredients

- 1 lb. ground chicken
- 8 oz spicy Italian sausage
- 1/4 onion - diced very small
- 1-1/2 tbsp minced garlic
- 6 small mushrooms - diced very small (about 1-1/2 cups)
- 2 eggs
- 2 tbsp fresh parsley - diced small
- 3 tbsp coconut flour
- 1 tsp salt
- 1 tsp pepper

For the sauce

- 1 tbsp apple cider vinegar
- 1/4 cup coconut aminos
- 1/4 cup Dijon mustard

- *1/4 tsp red pepper flakes*
- *1/2 tsp arrowroot flour*

Instructions

- Preheat your oven to 375 degrees F.
- Combine all the ingredients for the meatballs in a large bowl. Use your hands and make sure everything is mixed well.
- Shape the meat into small meatballs and place on a large baking sheet. I used about 1 tbsp for each meatball for a small appetizer style meatball.
- Once all the meatballs are in place, place the baking sheet in the oven to bake for 30 minutes.
- When the meatballs have about 10 minutes left to cook, start the sauce.
- Put a small saucepan over medium heat and add all the ingredients except the flour. Mix the sauce well and let heat.
- When the sauce is bubbling, add the flour. This thickens the sauce a bit, making it perfect for dipping. Reduce the heat to low and simmer the sauce until the meatballs are cooked.
- Serve meatballs and sauce with toothpicks for dipping.

NUTRITION FACTS (PER SERVING)		
Calories	91	
Total Fat	3g	4%
Saturated Fat	1.4g	7%
Cholesterol	21mg	7%
Sodium	206mg	9%
Total Carbohydrate	8.6g	3%
Dietary Fiber	0.8g	3%
Total Sugars	0.6g	
Protein	6.8g	

Tips: Meatballs need to be seasoned, period. As a rule, about 1 teaspoon per pound will make for perfectly salted meat.

TURKEY WINGS

Prep time: 5 min	Cook time: 1 hour 5 min	Servings: 4

Ingredients

- *2 pounds turkey wings*
- *1 tbsp coconut oil*
- *1 tsp sea salt*
- *1/4 tsp freshly ground black pepper*
- *2 tbsp almond butter*
- *2 tbsp honey*
- *1 tbsp coconut aminos*
- *1/4 tsp ground ginger*
- *pinch of cayenne pepper*

Instructions

- Preheat the oven to 400 ° F and place a wire rack on a large foil-lined baking sheet.
- Pat the turkey wings dry and place them in a large bowl with coconut oil, salt and pepper. Place the wings on the wire rack in a single layer and bake for 50 minutes until crispy and cooked through.
- When the wings have about five minutes left, make the frosting. Whisk the almond butter, honey, coconut amino, ground ginger and cayenne pepper in a small saucepan over medium heat for one to two minutes until thick and shiny.
- Transfer the cooked wings to a clean bowl, drizzle with the frosting and toss the wings to evenly coat them. Use tongs to put the wings back in the grill and cook for another ten minutes, until they sizzle and brown in places.
- Sprinkle the wings with chives and sesame seeds and serve hot.

NUTRITION FACTS (PER SERVING)

Calories	206	
Total Fat	12.9g	17%
Saturated Fat	3.3g	16%
Cholesterol	0mg	0%
Sodium	473mg	21%
Total Carbohydrate	11.1g	4%
Dietary Fiber	0.9g	3%
Total Sugars	9g	
Protein	13.3g	

Tips: High heat is required to really crisp up the outer skin on the turkey wing. If the wings are cooked at a low temperature, they will not crisp.

BUFFALO LAMB MEATBALLS

Prep time: 15 min	Cook time: 2 hours	Servings: 4

Ingredients

- *1 lb. ground lamb*
- *1/3 cup coconut flour*
- *1 egg*
- *2 cloves garlic, minced*
- *2 green onions, thinly sliced*
- *3/4 cup buffalo sauce*
- *sea salt and freshly ground black pepper*

Instructions

- Preheat your oven to 400 degrees F.
- In a bowl, combine the ground lamb, coconut flour, egg, garlic and onion and season with salt and pepper.

- Mix everything until everything is well combined.
- Roll the mixture into 1 or 1/2-inch meatballs.
- Place the meatballs on a baking sheet and bake in the preheated oven for 5 minutes.
- Turn off the oven and place the meatballs on a slow cooker. Add the buffalo sauce and toss to combine.
- Cover and simmer for 2 hours.
- Serve with ranch sauce for dipping (optional).

NUTRITION FACTS (PER SERVING)

Calories	177	
Total Fat	9.3g	12%
Saturated Fat	2.8g	14%
Cholesterol	96mg	32%
Sodium	357mg	16%
Total Carbohydrate	2.2g	1%
Dietary Fiber	0.8g	3%
Total Sugars	0.3g	
Protein	20.8g	

Tips: While you can make meatballs out of any ground meat, fattier meats like beef, lamb, and pork will yield more tender meatballs. If you use leaner meats like chicken or turkey, be careful not to overcook them or they can become tough. For great flavor, use a blend of different kinds of ground meats.

PARSNIPS STRIPS

Prep time: 10 min	Cook time: 50 min	Servings: 2

Ingredients

- 3 medium parsnips, peeled and cut into thin fry-like strips
- 3 tbsp almond butter
- 1 tbsp coconut oil
- 1/4 tsp kosher salt, or to taste

Instructions

- Preheat the oven to 400 ° F and line a baking sheet with parchment paper for easy cleanup. Peel the parsnips and cut them into roasted strips.
- In a medium bowl, whisk together the nut butter, coconut oil and salt. Take the parsnips and mix them in a bowl with your hands until they are completely covered. Place on a baking sheet and bake at 400F for 30 to 50 minutes until crispy.

NUTRITION FACTS (PER SERVING)		
Calories	128	
Total Fat	8.1g	10%
Saturated Fat	3.3g	17%
Cholesterol	0mg	0%
Sodium	79mg	3%
Total Carbohydrate	13.5g	5%
Dietary Fiber	4.1g	14%
Total Sugars	3.5g	
Protein	2.5g	

Tips: Parsnips are an excellent source of many important nutrients, packing a hearty dose of fiber, vitamins, and minerals into each serving.

FISH STICKS

Prep time: 15 min	Cook time: 15 min	Servings: 4

Ingredients

- 1 pound cod fish
- 1 cup coconut flour
- 1 tsp sea salt
- 1 tsp ground black pepper
- 1 tsp onion powder
- 1 tsp garlic powder
- 1 tsp paprika
- 1 tsp cumin
- 1 pastured egg, whisked
- 3-6 tbsp coconut oil

Instructions

- Combine coconut flour and spices in a large bowl with a whisk. (You can change the spices as you like and just omit or add the spices you like the most.) Set aside.
- Cut the fish into pieces the size of fish sticks and set aside.
- Beat the egg in a small bowl. Cover each piece of fish with the beaten egg, then the dough and set aside near the oven.
- Heat 3 tablespoons of coconut oil on the stovetop in a large skillet over medium heat until you can pour a small drop of water into the pot and sizzle.
- Once the oil is hot, carefully place half the fish fingers in the pan, making sure they are not touching each other.
- Cook for a few minutes on each side until golden brown on each side, turning them very carefully with tongs.
- When it's nice and golden on both sides, remove it and place it on a paper towel-lined plate.
- If your pan is particularly crisp from the first batch, allow it to cool and drain the oil and any leftover dough.
- Add the remaining 3 tablespoons of coconut oil to your pan and repeat the process for the second half of the fish fingers.
- Serve with a paleo-friendly tomato sauce!

NUTRITION FACTS (PER SERVING)

Calories	266	
Total Fat	17.9g	23%
Saturated Fat	10.4g	52%
Cholesterol	50mg	17%
Sodium	536mg	23%
Total Carbohydrate	3.9g	1%
Dietary Fiber	1.8g	6%
Total Sugars	0.8g	
Protein	23.8g	

Tips: A white, firm fish is best for fish sticks. Cod or haddock fillets are the best option, but tilapia will work. Just keep in mind they are a bit thinner than cod or haddock and may not need to be cooked as long.

PUMPKIN SOUP

Prep time: 10 min	Cook time: 15 min	Servings: 6

Ingredients

- *1 tbsp coconut oil*
- *1 medium onion, chopped*
- *1 large carrot, chopped*
- *1 leek, chopped*
- *3 cloves of garlic, minced*
- *1 medium sized squash*
- *3 cups vegetable broth*
- *1 green apple, peeled, cored, and chopped*
- *1/4 tsp ground cinnamon*
- *1 sprig fresh thyme*
- *1 sprig fresh rosemary*

- *1 tsp kosher salt*
- *1/4 tsp black pepper*
- *pinch of nutmeg, optional*

Instructions

- Choose to sauté in your Instant Pot. Add coconut oil and sauté onion, carrot, leek and garlic for about 3 to 5 minutes. Add the vegetable broth, pumpkin, apple, cinnamon, thyme, rosemary, salt, pepper and nutmeg if using.
- Place the lid securely on the Instant Pot and turn the knob to close it. Cook under high pressure for 10 minutes and quickly release the pressure.
- Use a hand blender in the instant pot to puree the soup until smooth. If you don't have a hand blender, you can let the soup cool slightly and gently put it in a regular blender and stir until smooth.
- Serve the soup in bowls and serve lukewarm.

NUTRITION FACTS (PER SERVING)

Calories	142	
Total Fat	3.4g	4%
Saturated Fat	2.3g	11%
Cholesterol	0mg	0%
Sodium	784mg	34%
Total Carbohydrate	26.2g	10%
Dietary Fiber	3.3g	12%
Total Sugars	9.3g	
Protein	5.5g	

Tips: Since an Instant Pot shoots steam straight up, it's always best to use it in an unobstructed or well-circulated place, like under a hood vent. Avoid releasing steam right under cabinets — because repeated exposure to heat and steam can mess with wood and paint.

ZUCCHINI PASTA SALAD

Prep time: 15 min	Cook time: 0 min	Servings: 4

Ingredients

- 4 medium zucchini spiralized
- 2 cups grape tomatoes sliced in half
- 1 cup red onion diced
- 1 cup brussels sprouts chopped
- 1 green bell pepper diced

For the dressing

- 4 tbsp extra virgin olive oil
- 2 tbsp balsamic vinegar
- 2 tbsp lemon juice

- *2 tbsp minced garlic*
- *3 tbsp basil*

Instructions

- In a bowl, combine the dressing ingredients. Put aside.
- In another large bowl, toss the vegetables for the salad. Drizzle with dressing and serve.
- If not served immediately, keep the dressing separate from the salad until you are ready to eat it.

NUTRITION FACTS (PER SERVING)		
Calories	143	
Total Fat	7.8g	10%
Saturated Fat	1.2g	6%
Cholesterol	0mg	0%
Sodium	35mg	2%
Total Carbohydrate	17.7g	6%
Dietary Fiber	5.5g	20%
Total Sugars	8.5g	
Protein	4.9g	

Tip: Zucchini is packed with many important vitamins, minerals, and antioxidants. It has a high fiber content and a low-calorie count.

BAKED SALMON WITH QUINOA

Prep time: 10 min	Cook time: 20 min	Servings: 4

Ingredients

- *4 (4 oz.) salmon fillets*
- *1 cup quinoa*
- *2 cups water*
- *½ cup broccoli*
- *3 tbsp dried cranberries*
- *1 tsp garlic minced*
- *1/2 tsp salt*
- *1/4 tsp pepper*
- *1 tbsp lime zest*
- *fresh basil or cilantro for garnish*

Instructions

- Prepare quinoa. Put 1 cup of quinoa in a pot with 2 cups of water or boil 2 cups of water on the stove, add quinoa and salt. Simmer for about 30 to 35 minutes until the quinoa is tender.
- Preheat the oven to 400 degrees. Sprinkle the salmon with garlic, salt and pepper. Place on a baking sheet and bake for about 15-20 minutes.
- When the quinoa is ready, immediately stir in the broccoli, cranberries, salt and pepper. Put the salmon on it and add the lime zest. Salt and pepper to taste.
- Garnish with basil or cilantro.

NUTRITION FACTS (PER SERVING)		
Calories	315	
Total Fat	9.6g	12%
Saturated Fat	1.3g	7%
Cholesterol	50mg	17%
Sodium	351mg	15%
Total Carbohydrate	29.1g	11%
Dietary Fiber	3.7g	13%
Total Sugars	0.5g	
Protein	28.4g	

Tip: Chicken, beef or vegetable stock or broth can be substituted for water to add more flavor the quinoa.

ROASTED RED PEPPER TOMATO SOUP

Prep time: 15 min	Cook time: 30 min	Servings: 4

Ingredients

- *3 red bell peppers quartered*
- *1-pound plum tomatoes quartered*
- *1 yellow onion quartered*
- *4 large garlic cloves*
- *1 tbsp coconut or olive oil*
- *1/2 tsp dry parsley*
- *1/2 tsp dry basil*
- *3 cups low sodium vegetable broth*
- *1/4 cup raw almond*
- *salt and pepper to taste*

Instructions

- Preheat oven to 425 degrees F (convection baking) and line a large baking sheet with parchment paper. Arrange your vegetables in a single layer and drizzle with oil (if using) and sprinkle with parsley and basil.
- Roast the vegetables for 30 to 40 minutes or until the skin of the pepper is blackened, then take them out of the oven. Once cool to the touch, peel the peppers. The skins peel off easily, but if there are any stubborn lumps, leave them.
- Peel the garlic, it comes out easily after roasting. Put in your blender with all the other ingredients except the sides. Stir everything until smooth, season with salt and pepper and adjust if necessary.
- Serve garnished with fresh basil, croutons, crackers or black pepper.

NUTRITION FACTS (PER SERVING)

Calories	116	
Total Fat	6.4g	8%
Saturated Fat	3.2g	16%
Cholesterol	0mg	0%
Sodium	329mg	14%
Total Carbohydrate	14.1g	5%
Dietary Fiber	3.3g	12%
Total Sugars	7g	
Protein	2.7g	

Tips: Leftovers can be kept refrigerated for up to 4 days, or you can freeze them in a freezer safe, air tight container for up to 3 months.

STIR FRY WITH CHICKEN AND CAULIFLOWER

Prep time: 10 min	Cook time: 20 min	Servings: 4

Ingredients

- *3 cups cauliflower florets*
- *1 tbsp coconut oil*
- *2 skinless, boneless chicken breast halves - cut into 1-inch strips*
- *1/4 cup sliced green onions*
- *4 cloves garlic, thinly sliced*
- *1 tbsp hoisin sauce*
- *1 tbsp chile paste*
- *1 tbsp low sodium soy sauce*
- *1/2 tsp ground ginger*
- *1/4 tsp crushed red pepper*
- *1/2 tsp salt*
- *1/2 tsp black pepper*
- *1/8 cup chicken stock*

Instructions

- Place the cauliflower in a steamer with over 1 inch of boiling water and cover. Cook for 5 minutes, until tender but still firm.
- In a skillet, heat the oil over medium heat and brown the chicken, spring onions and garlic until the chicken is no longer pink and the juices run clear.
- Stir in hoisin sauce, chili paste and soy sauce in skillet. Season with ginger, red pepper, salt and black pepper. Add the chicken broth and simmer for about 2 minutes. Add the steamed cauliflower until coated with the sauce mixture.

NUTRITION FACTS (PER SERVING)

Calories	154	
Total Fat	6.3g	8%
Saturated Fat	3.7g	19%
Cholesterol	34mg	11%
Sodium	672mg	29%
Total Carbohydrate	9.5g	3%
Dietary Fiber	2.4g	9%
Total Sugars	4.2g	
Protein	16g	

Tips: Of the 100 grams of cauliflower in one serving, 92 grams are water. This means this veggie can help keep you hydrated and you can eat a lot of it. It's also a good source of fiber

TOFU LETTUCE WRAPS WITH PEANUT SAUCE

| Prep time: 10 min | Cook time: 20 min | Servings: 4 |

Ingredients

- 4-ounce block of tofu
- 1/2 cup vegetable broth
- 1/2 tsp soy sauce
- 1/2 tsp maple syrup
- 1/8 tsp ground coriander
- 1/8 tsp garlic powder
- 4 leaves of butter lettuce
- 1 small carrot, peeled and julienned
- 1 to 1 1/2 cups thinly sliced cabbage
- 1 medium red bell pepper, sliced
- peanut sauce

Garnish

- *1 stalk of scallions, sliced (optional)*
- *red pepper flakes (optional)*

Instructions

- Cut the tofu into ½-inch cubes and place in a food processor. Blend the tofu for about 5 seconds until you get very small pieces.
- In a bowl, combine the vegetable broth, soy sauce, maple syrup, garlic powder and ground cilantro.
- Heat a coated skillet or frying pan over medium heat. Add the tofu broth mixture.
- Cook, stirring occasionally, 8 to 9 minutes, until the liquids are completely absorbed by the tofu. It may seem like the tofu is ready to be removed from the stove in 5 minutes, but resist the urge to do so.
- Once the liquid has been absorbed, remove the saucepan from the heat.
- Assemble the salad buns. Stuff the lettuce leaves with carrots, cabbage, red pepper and tofu. Pour peanut sauce over filling and garnish with sliced chives and paprika flakes, if desired. Use immediately.

NUTRITION FACTS (PER SERVING)

Calories	101	
Total Fat	4.2g	5%
Saturated Fat	0.8g	4%
Cholesterol	0mg	0%
Sodium	216mg	9%
Total Carbohydrate	10.1g	4%
Dietary Fiber	1.5g	5%
Total Sugars	4.7g	
Protein	7.1g	

Tips: The great thing about lettuce wraps is that they are easily modifiable when it comes to the filling and the wrapping. Cabbage leaves would also be a yummy substitute.

4. DESSERT RECIPES

ALMOND BUTTER BALLS

Prep time: 5 min	Cook time: 0 min	Servings: 16 balls

Ingredients

- 1 cup almond butter
- 1/3 cup almond flour
- 1 1/2 cup chocolate chips
- optional toppings: sprinkles, chopped nuts, etc.

Instructions

- Line a baking sheet with baking paper.
- Wisk together almond butter and almond flour in a bowl. A thick paste should form after a few minutes.
- Shape a large tbsp of the mixture into a ball and place it on a baking sheet. Once all balls are done, place the baking sheet in the freezer for 10-15 min.
- Melt chocolate chips on a medium low heat or in a microwave.
- Using a spoon or a fork, dip the chilled almond butter balls into the melted chocolate, making sure it's completely covered.
- Return the balls to the baking sheet and sprinkle with toppings, while the chocolate is still soft.
- Place the balls in the freezer until the chocolate has hardened.

NUTRITION FACTS (PER SERVING)

Calories	94	
Total Fat	5.9g	8%
Saturated Fat	3g	15%
Cholesterol	3mg	1%
Sodium	11mg	0%
Total Carbohydrate	9g	3%
Dietary Fiber	0.8g	3%
Total Sugars	7.3g	
Protein	1.8g	

Tips: Almond butter is slightly healthier than peanut butter because it has more vitamins, minerals, and fiber. Both nut butters are roughly equal in calories and sugar, but peanut butter has a little more protein than almond butter.

FUDGE

Prep time: 15 min	Cook time: 60 min	Servings: 10

Ingredients

- *1/2 cup coconut oil, softened or melted*
- *1/2 cup almond butter*
- *3/4 cup unsweetened cocoa powder*
- *1/4 cup + 1 tbsp honey*
- *1/4 tsp vanilla extract*
- *1/8 tsp sea salt or to taste*

Instructions

- Line a square tray with parchment paper. The size will depend on the thickness or fineness of your fudge.
- In a medium bowl, combine all the ingredients until smooth.
- Pour the mixture into the pot and use a spatula to spread it evenly.
- Place in the refrigerator until they set, about 2-3 hours.
- Once it's done, you can sprinkle it with more salt or coconut flakes.
- Cut into squares. It's a rich fudge so you can keep it smaller if you want. Keep refrigerated.

NUTRITION FACTS (PER SERVING)

Calories	142	
Total Fat	12.2g	16%
Saturated Fat	10.8g	54%
Cholesterol	0mg	0%
Sodium	26mg	1%
Total Carbohydrate	10.7g	4%
Dietary Fiber	2.2g	8%
Total Sugars	7.1g	
Protein	1.5g	

Tips: Some fudge needs to be stored in the refrigerator, while others require it to be stored in a cool, dry place. Coverings can consist of aluminum foil, plastic wrap, resealable bags, or containers. Fudge can be stored in the refrigerator for up to 2 weeks and in the freezer for about 3 months.

SWEET CARROT CAKE

| Prep time: 30 min | Cook time: 50 min | Servings: 3 |

Ingredients

- *3 eggs*
- *3 tbsp honey*
- *1 carrot*
- *zest of 1/2 orange*
- *juice of 1/4 orange*
- *1 1/2 cups coconut flour*

Instructions

- Preheat the oven to 325 F. Separate egg whites and yolks.
- Put the carrot in a pot of boiling water and cook until the carrots are tender. Drain it and mash it with a food processor of forks.
- Mix the carrot puree with the orange zest, orange juice and coconut flour.
- In another bowl, beat the egg yolks and honey and mix with the carrot and flour mixture.
- In another bowl, beat the egg whites into snow. Using a spatula, gently fold the snow into the flour mixture.
- Grease a 9-inch round cake pan and pour batter into it.
- Bake for about 50 minutes.
- Let cool for 15 minutes before opening the feather pan so that the cake does not stick.
- Cut into pieces and serve hot.

NUTRITION FACTS (PER SERVING)

Calories	198	
Total Fat	6.5g	8%
Saturated Fat	2.9g	14%
Cholesterol	196mg	65%
Sodium	114mg	5%
Total Carbohydrate	27.2g	10%
Dietary Fiber	4.3g	16%
Total Sugars	19.2g	
Protein	8.3g	

Tips: Use real food to naturally color your frosting for cake and cookies. You know when the cake is cooked, when the toothpick inserted in the middle of it, comes out clean.

APPLE PIE MUFFINS

| Prep time: 20 min | Cook time: 25 min | Servings: 4 |

Ingredients

- *1 cup coconut flour*
- *1/2 cup almond flour*
- *1 1/2 cups apples, sliced or chopped*
- *1 tsp baking soda*
- *2 tsp ground nutmeg*
- *4 eggs, beaten*
- *1 cup homemade applesauce*
- *2 tsp vanilla extract*
- *2 tbsp coconut oil, melted*
- *1/4 cup sliced walnut*

Instructions

- Preheat the oven to 375 F.
- Combine all the ingredients (except the almonds) with half the sliced apples in a bowl and stir until combined.
- Pour the mixture evenly into the muffin pan.
- Top each muffin with the remaining sliced apples and sprinkle with almonds.
- Bake in preheated oven for 20 to 25 minutes or until firm and a toothpick inserted in center comes out clean.

NUTRITION FACTS (PER SERVING)		
Calories	293	
Total Fat	19.2g	25%
Saturated Fat	4.9g	24%
Cholesterol	164mg	55%
Sodium	385mg	17%
Total Carbohydrate	22g	8%
Dietary Fiber	6.1g	22%
Total Sugars	14.2g	
Protein	11.1g	

Tips: Use a cheese shredder to shred your apple and shred the skin as well. There is a lot of good fiber in the skin so don't miss out on.

BANANA BREAD

Prep time: 10 min	Cook time: 40 min	Servings: 6

Ingredients

- 1 cup hazelnut butter or cashew nut butter
- 1 cup coconut flour
- 3 bananas, very ripe
- 2 eggs
- 1 tsp baking powder
- 1 tsp baking soda

Instructions

- Preheat the oven to 350 F.
- In a bowl, mash the bananas with a fork and add the hazelnut butter, coconut flour and the eggs. Mix well.
- Then add the baking soda and baking soda and mix well.
- Place in a lightly greased 9x5 loaf pan and bake for about 35 to 40 minutes, until a toothpick inserted in the middle comes out clean.

NUTRITION FACTS (PER SERVING)

Calories	324	
Total Fat	25.9g	33%
Saturated Fat	2.7g	14%
Cholesterol	55mg	18%
Sodium	238mg	10%
Total Carbohydrate	21.6g	8%
Dietary Fiber	6.2g	22%
Total Sugars	8.8g	
Protein	9.1g	

Tips: You can replace banana puree with applesauce without having to worry about adding or cutting out ingredients such as sugar or fat.

CHOCOLATE FAT BOMBS

Prep time: 10 min	Cook time: 0 min	Servings: 24 pieces

Ingredients

- *1 cup coconut oil, melted*
- *1/2 cup cocoa powder*
- *1 cup cashew nut butter*
- *1 tsp vanilla*
- *pinch of salt*

Instructions

- Combine all the ingredients in a blender and stir until smooth.
- To mix in the small molds of your choice.
- Put in the refrigerator and let stand for at least 2 hours.
- Once it's ready, put it in an airtight container and store in the fridge for up to 2 weeks.

NUTRITION FACTS (PER SERVING)		
Calories	92	
Total Fat	10.1g	13%
Saturated Fat	8.2g	41%
Cholesterol	0mg	0%
Sodium	9mg	0%
Total Carbohydrate	1.4g	1%
Dietary Fiber	0.6g	2%
Total Sugars	0.1g	
Protein	0.5g	

Tips: Fat bombs must be stored in the freezer, as they will be too soft in the fridge or at room temperature.

SWEET POTATO BROWNIES

Prep time: 20 min	Cook time: 25 min	Servings: 4

Ingredients

- 1 cup sweet potato puree
- 1 cup creamy peanut butter
- 1/4 cup dark cocoa powder
- 1 tsp pure vanilla extract
- 1/4 cup sliced pecans

Instructions

- Preheat the oven to 350 F.
- Melt the peanut butter in a saucepan over low heat.
- In a bowl, combine the mashed sweet potatoes, melted peanut butter, cocoa powder and vanilla extract.
- Toss until well blended and pour into greased 8 x 8-inch pan.
- Cover the mixture with the chopped pecans and put in the oven.
- Bake in preheated oven 20 to 25 minutes or until no longer runny.
- Let the brownies cool completely before slicing them.

NUTRITION FACTS (PER SERVING)

Calories	226	
Total Fat	16.6g	21%
Saturated Fat	3.5g	17%
Cholesterol	0mg	0%
Sodium	172mg	7%
Total Carbohydrate	13.9g	5%
Dietary Fiber	2.5g	9%
Total Sugars	4.9g	
Protein	8.7g	

Tips: A single sweet potato can contain 769 percent of the amount of Vitamin A you need to consume daily. Vitamin A is great for your vision, bones and skin, and helps strengthen your immune system.

CHOCOLATE ALMOND BALLS

Prep time: 20 min	Cook time: 25 min	Servings: 4

Ingredients

- *1 cup roasted almonds, roughly chopped*
- *10 whole roasted almonds*
- *2 tbsp raw cocoa powder*
- *1 tsp pure vanilla extract*
- *1/4 cup honey*

Instructions

- In a food processor, combine half a cup of chopped almond until smooth.
- Add the honey, cocoa powder and vanilla extract.
- Mix again until everything is smooth and sticky.
- Roll the 10-whole almond in the chocolate-almond mixture. Dip them in the rest of the chopped almond.
- Place on a baking sheet lined with parchment paper.
- Place in the freezer for 15 to 20 minutes. Remove 4 to 5 minutes before eating.

NUTRITION FACTS (PER SERVING)

Calories	256	
Total Fat	16g	20%
Saturated Fat	1.4g	7%
Cholesterol	0mg	0%
Sodium	2mg	0%
Total Carbohydrate	25.7g	9%
Dietary Fiber	4.8g	17%
Total Sugars	18.6g	
Protein	7.1g	

Tips: almonds are the most packed with nutrients and beneficial components. Now all you need to do is to at about 8-10 almonds a day.

FLOURLESS CHOCOLATE CAKES

Prep time: 15 min	Cook time: 30 min	Servings: 2

Ingredients

- 2 ripe bananas
- 1 egg, beaten
- 2 tbsp maple syrup
- 3 to 4 tbsp dark cocoa powder
- 1/4 tsp pure vanilla extract
- 2 tbsp sliced walnuts

Instructions

- Preheat the oven to 375 F.
- Combine all the ingredients (except the walnuts slices) in a blender until smooth.
- Pour the mixer into 2 cups; Garnish with slivered walnuts.
- Place in the oven and bake for 25 to 30 minutes.
- Let the cake rest 3 to 5 minutes before serving.

NUTRITION FACTS (PER SERVING)		
Calories	238	
Total Fat	7.2g	9%
Saturated Fat	1.1g	5%
Cholesterol	82mg	27%
Sodium	34mg	1%
Total Carbohydrate	41.4g	15%
Dietary Fiber	3.6g	13%
Total Sugars	26.7g	
Protein	5.9g	

Tips: Unfrosted cupcakes are wonderful left at room temperature for a few days. Cover them tightly and they'll stay soft, moist, and fluffy until you're ready to decorate them.

DRIED FRUIT BARS

| Prep time: 15 min | Cook time: 10 min | Servings: 4 |

Ingredients

- *1 cup dried Medjool dates, pitted*
- *1/2 cup raw almonds*
- *1/2 cup cashew*
- *1/2 cup dried cranberries*
- *1/2 cup dried blueberries*

Instructions

- Preheat your oven to 400 F.
- Place the almonds, cashew in a baking dish and bake for 8-10 minutes. Let cool before use.
- In a food processor, combine all the ingredients and squeeze until the ingredients form a ball. Scrape the edges of the bowl to prevent the mixture from sticking.
- Line a baking sheet with parchment paper. Distribute the mixture in the saucepan and form a large rectangle.
- Cover with another piece of parchment paper and refrigerate for at least 1 hour.
- Cut evenly into bars.

NUTRITION FACTS (PER SERVING)		
Calories	166	
Total Fat	10g	13%
Saturated Fat	1.2g	6%
Cholesterol	0mg	0%
Sodium	2mg	0%
Total Carbohydrate	19.5g	7%
Dietary Fiber	3.4g	12%
Total Sugars	10.5g	
Protein	4.2g	

Tips: Store in the refrigerator in an air tight container and refrigerate up to 2 weeks.

CHOCOLATE AVOCADO BANANA COOKIES

| Prep time: 15 min | Cook time: 10 min | Servings: 4 |

Ingredients

- *1 cup very ripe avocado flesh*
- *1 banana*
- *1 egg*
- *1/2 cup dark cocoa powder*
- *2 tbsp maple syrup*
- *dark chocolate chunks, to taste*
- *1/2 tsp baking soda*

Instructions

- Preheat your oven to 350 F.
- Combine the banana, avocado and maple syrup in a bowl.
- Mix everything together with a hand mixer or food processor until smooth.
- Add the egg, baking soda and cocoa powder and continue to mix until well combined.
- Add the dark chocolate pieces if you use them.
- Place cookie dough balls on a baking sheet lined with parchment paper. The dough will be very soft.
- Bake 8 to 10 minutes or until cookies are hot and firm.

NUTRITION FACTS (PER SERVING)		
Calories	113	
Total Fat	6.8g	9%
Saturated Fat	1.6g	8%
Cholesterol	22mg	7%
Sodium	100mg	4%
Total Carbohydrate	14.7g	5%
Dietary Fiber	4.1g	15%
Total Sugars	6.3g	
Protein	2.5g	

Tips: Once the cookies are completely cool, store them in an airtight container at room temperature for up to 4 days. You can also store these cookies in the freezer for up to 1 month. Keep in a zipper-top freezer back then let them thaw for 30 minutes at room temperature before eating.

COCONUT DATE BALLS

| Prep time: 15 min | Cook time: 5 min | Servings: 4 |

Ingredients

- *1 cup dates, roughly chopped*
- *2 eggs, beaten*
- *1/2 cup Maple syrup*
- *1 tsp vanilla extract*
- *1/4 cup coconut oil*
- *2 cups walnuts, chopped small*
- *1 cup coconut flakes*
- *1/2 tsp sea salt*

Instructions

- Combine eggs, coconut oil, maple syrup and dates in a medium saucepan over medium heat.
- Bring everything to a boil for 3 to 5 minutes, stirring occasionally.
- Remove from the heat, add the vanilla and sea salt.
- Add the chopped walnuts and stir until combined.
- Roll the mixture into balls.
- Roll each ball in coconut flakes until well covered.
- Cool to firm and serve.

NUTRITION FACTS (PER SERVING)		
Calories	296	
Total Fat	23.8g	31%
Saturated Fat	8.2g	41%
Cholesterol	33mg	11%
Sodium	109mg	5%
Total Carbohydrate	17.9g	6%
Dietary Fiber	3.8g	14%
Total Sugars	12.8g	
Protein	7.8g	

Tips: you can store them in the fridge or freezer! Fridge storage- portion out energy bites into a 4-6 cup meal prep container and store in the fridge for up to 1 week.

COCONUT MILK CUSTARD

Prep time: 15 min	Cook time: 40 min	Servings: 6

Ingredients

- 5 eggs
- 2 tsp vanilla extract
- 2 cups unsweetened coconut milk
- 1/4 cup maple syrup
- hot water
- cinnamon and nutmeg to taste, for garnishing

Instructions

- Preheat the oven to 325 F.
- Heat the coconut milk and maple syrup in a saucepan; bring to a boil.
- Remove from heat after cooking.
- In a bowl, whisk the eggs and vanilla until combined and smooth.
- Slowly stir the hot coconut milk into the egg mixture, being careful not to boil the eggs.
- Pour the mixture into 6 individual baking dishes and place them in a baking dish.
- Fill the baking dish with hot water to the same level as the pudding in the shapes and place in the oven to bake for about 40 minutes until the edges are firm.
- Refrigerate for about 2 hours before serving. Sprinkle with cinnamon and nutmeg just before serving.

NUTRITION FACTS (PER SERVING)

Calories	99	
Total Fat	4.4g	6%
Saturated Fat	1.8g	9%
Cholesterol	136mg	45%
Sodium	53mg	2%
Total Carbohydrate	9.9g	4%
Dietary Fiber	0.4g	1%
Total Sugars	8.3g	
Protein	4.6g	

Tips: If the eggs aren't cooked enough, proteins don't cross-link enough to disrupt the flow of water, and the custard is thin and runny. Should they be overcooked, the proteins in the eggs begin to coagulate tightly, forming small curds.

BLUEBERRY COBBLER

Prep time: 15 min	Cook time: 45 min	Servings: 4

Ingredients

- *1 cup almond flour*
- *2/3 cup tapioca flour*
- *1/3 cup coconut flour*
- *3 tsp baking powder*
- *1/2 tsp salt*
- *1 tablespoon coconut oil, melted*
- *1/4 cup honey*
- *2 cups unsweetened almond milk*
- *1 cup. fresh blueberries*

Instructions

- Preheat the oven to 350 F.
- Sift together the almond flour, tapioca flour and coconut flour in a medium bowl.
- Add the baking soda and salt.
- Next, mix honey and milk, then add the melted coconut oil.
- Beat in a baking dish.
- Distribute the berries evenly over the dough and place in the oven.
- Bake for 40 to 45 minutes until the mixture is bubbling.

NUTRITION FACTS (PER SERVING)		
Calories	173	
Total Fat	6.7g	9%
Saturated Fat	1.6g	8%
Cholesterol	0mg	0%
Sodium	389mg	17%
Total Carbohydrate	28.2g	10%
Dietary Fiber	2.8g	10%
Total Sugars	6.8g	
Protein	2.5g	

Tips: Store the cobbler at room temperature for as long as three days.

BANANA APRICOTS COOKIES

Prep time: 5 min	Cook time: 30 min	Servings: 4

Ingredients

- 3 ripe bananas
- 1/4 cup applesauce
- 3 cups almond meal
- 1/2 cup coconut flour
- 1/4 cup coconut flakes;
- 1/4 cup full-fat coconut milk
- 1/2 cup apricot
- 1 tsp vanilla
- 1 tsp cinnamon

Instructions

- Preheat your oven to 350 F.
- In a large bowl, mash the bananas until mashed. Then add the rest of the ingredients and stir until smooth.
- We have a pan covered with parchment or lightly greased. Consider a tablespoon of the cookie mixture.
- Place the baking sheet in the oven and bake for 25 to 30 minutes, or until golden brown.
- Serve hot.

NUTRITION FACTS (PER SERVING)		
Calories	124	
Total Fat	9.2g	12%
Saturated Fat	1.3g	6%
Cholesterol	0mg	0%
Sodium	2mg	0%
Total Carbohydrate	8.9g	3%
Dietary Fiber	2.6g	9%
Total Sugars	3.6g	
Protein	4g	

Tips: Store in airtight container at room temperature for up to 5 days. You can freeze cookies too! Slide baked cookies into Ziploc freezer bag and squeeze out excess air. Store in freezer for up to 3 months.

ALMOND TAPIOCA PUDDING

Prep time: 20 min	Cook time: 35 min	Servings: 6

Ingredients

- 1/2 cup small tapioca pearls
- 2.5 cans unsweetened almond milk
- 1 vanilla bean
- 2 large egg yolks
- 3 tbsp maple syrup

Instructions

- Combine the tapioca, almond milk and the vanilla bean in a large saucepan over medium heat.
- Bring to a boil and cook, stirring occasionally, until the tapioca is translucent and tender (about 20 minutes). Stir in the rest of the coconut milk.
- In a small bowl, combine the egg yolks with the maple syrup until smooth. Very slowly pour in about half a cup of hot almond while continuing to whisk. Take your time with this step or you will get scrambled eggs! Then pour the egg and almond mixture into the pot, stirring constantly, and continue stirring for about 5 minutes.
- Cool the pudding and serve cold.

NUTRITION FACTS (PER SERVING)

Calories	131	
Total Fat	3.6g	5%
Saturated Fat	1g	5%
Cholesterol	73mg	24%
Sodium	86mg	4%
Total Carbohydrate	23.6g	9%
Dietary Fiber	0.4g	2%
Total Sugars	7.8g	
Protein	1.8g	

Tips: It's easy to over-cook tapioca so even if the pudding looks runny, pull it off the heat. It will definitely get thicker as it cools.

FRUIT CAKE

| Prep time: 15 min | Cook time: 60 min | Servings: 6 |

Ingredients

- 1 1/2 cups almond flour
- 1/2 cup coconut flour
- 1/2 tsp baking powder
- 5 eggs
- 1 cup coconut sugar
- 1/4 cup coconut oil
- 1 tsp ground cloves
- 1 tsp ground cinnamon
- 1 tsp ground nutmeg
- 1 tsp vanilla extract
- 1 cup dates, chopped
- 2 cups raisins

- *1 cup dried cherries*
- *1 cup assorted dry fruits of your choice (mango, apricots, cranberry)*
- *1/2 tsp sea salt*

Instructions

- Preheat your oven to 350 F.
- In a large bowl, combine the almond flour, coconut flour, salt and baking powder.
- Add the ground cloves, cinnamon and nutmeg to the almond flour and mix again.
- In another bowl, combine the eggs, butter, coconut sugar and vanilla.
- Stir the wet ingredients into the dry ingredients and mix until smooth.
- Add the dried fruits to the mixture and stir again.
- Pour the mixture into a greased loaf pan and bake for 45 minutes. up to 1 hour.

NUTRITION FACTS (PER SERVING)		
Calories	199	
Total Fat	8.2g	11%
Saturated Fat	3.1g	16%
Cholesterol	41mg	14%
Sodium	66mg	3%
Total Carbohydrate	31.2g	11%
Dietary Fiber	2.4g	9%
Total Sugars	24.3g	
Protein	3.9g	

Tips: Be sure to grease and flour pans or use greased brown paper for liners. Greased wax paper is also used in some recipes.

FRIED BANANA

Prep time: 5 min	Cook time: 5 min	Servings: 1

Ingredients

- *1 banana, sliced*
- *1 tbsp maple syrup*
- *cinnamon (optional)*
- *2 tbsp coconut oil*

Instructions

- Mix maple syrup with 1/4 cup of lukewarm water and mix well.
- Heat the coconut oil in a skillet over medium to high heat.
- Put the banana slices in the pan and fry them for 2 minutes on each side.
- Remove the pan from the heat and pour in the maple syrup mixture.
- Sprinkle with cinnamon and serve.

NUTRITION FACTS (PER SERVING)		
Calories	196	
Total Fat	4.9g	6%
Saturated Fat	4g	20%
Cholesterol	0mg	0%
Sodium	3mg	0%
Total Carbohydrate	40.4g	15%
Dietary Fiber	3.1g	11%
Total Sugars	26.3g	
Protein	1.3g	

Tips: Cut the banana in half and then cut across into chunks. Heat the oil in a pan over high heat. Dip the bananas into the batter and try to coat them evenly.

PECANS AND COCONUT MACAROONS

Prep time: 15 min	Cook time: 12 min	Servings: 4

Ingredients

- *2 egg whites*
- *2 cups unsweetened shredded coconut*
- *1/4 cup maple syrup*
- *1/2 cup whole pecans, chopped into tiny pieces*
- *1 tsp pure vanilla extract*

Instructions

- Preheat your oven to 350 ° F.
- Line a baking sheet with parchment paper.
- In a large bowl, combine maple syrup and egg white.
- Add the pecans, dried coconut and vanilla to the bowl and mix everything together.
- Shape individual macaroni with the dough. Place each cookie on the prepared dish and place it in the oven.
- Bake the macaroni in the oven for about 12 minutes, until the base is golden brown.

NUTRITION FACTS (PER SERVING)

Calories	217	
Total Fat	19g	24%
Saturated Fat	9g	45%
Cholesterol	0mg	0%
Sodium	22mg	1%
Total Carbohydrate	9.1g	3%
Dietary Fiber	4g	14%
Total Sugars	4.7g	
Protein	4.3g	

Tips: A disposable piping bag makes things easy but you can use a Ziplock bag-just make sure you have a nice round circle so your batter comes out round not as a triangle.

CHOCOLATE PUDDING

Prep time: 15 min	Cook time: 12 min	Servings: 6

Ingredients

- *3 medium avocados*
- *1/4 cup maple syrup*
- *1/4 cup cocoa powder*
- *3 tbsp almond butter*
- *1 tsp lemon juice*
- *1 tsp ground cinnamon*
- *1 tsp ground nutmeg*
- *1/2 tsp mint extract*

Instructions

- Place everything in a large bowl and mix with a stand mixer or hand mixer. Of course, you can also use a blender or food processor for this job. I leave my mixture smooth and ready to eat.
- Put any leftovers in the fridge. Enjoy!

NUTRITION FACTS (PER SERVING)

Calories	239	
Total Fat	18.5g	24%
Saturated Fat	2.6g	13%
Cholesterol 0	mg	0%
Sodium	9mg	0%
Total Carbohydrate	20.3g	7%
Dietary Fiber	8.2g	29%
Total Sugars	8.7g	
Protein	4.1g	

Tips: Resist the urge to eat the luscious dessert warm. Yes, it's perfect. You succeeded in mastering homemade pudding but wait a little longer.

CHOCOLATE ORANGES

Prep time: 15 min	Cook time: 30 min	Servings: 6

Ingredients

- 5 mandarin, clementine or oranges, peeled
- 1/2 cup dark chocolate
- sea salt

Instructions

- Line a baking sheet with parchment paper.
- Melt the chocolate in a double boiler over boiling water over medium heat.
- Half-dip each orange slice in the melted chocolate and place it on the baking sheet.
- Sprinkle each chocolate-coated orange slice with sea salt, if using.
- Store in the refrigerator for 10 minutes and serve.

NUTRITION FACTS (PER SERVING)		
Calories	147	
Total Fat	4.3g	6%
Saturated Fat	2.9g	15%
Cholesterol	3mg	1%
Sodium	89mg	4%
Total Carbohydrate	26.3g	10%
Dietary Fiber	4.2g	15%
Total Sugars	21.6g	
Protein	2.5g	

Tips: Dark chocolate is bitter, meaning it matches well with fruit that is extra sweet (bananas, mango, figs, strawberries, etc.).

FRESH FRUIT POPSICLES

Prep time: 10 min	Cook time: 0 min	Servings: 6

Ingredients

- 2 kiwis, peeled and sliced
- 1 package fresh strawberries, sliced
- 1 package fresh raspberries
- 1 package fresh blueberries
- coconut water
- popsicle molds

Instructions

- Fill each popsicle mold with fresh fruit, but do not over tighten. You want some space in the center to fill it with coconut water.
- Fill each shape with coconut water.
- Freeze the mussels for at least 5 hours or until they are solid.

NUTRITION FACTS (PER SERVING)

Calories	45	
Total Fat	0.4g	0%
Saturated Fat	0.1g	0%
Cholesterol	0mg	0%
Sodium	43mg	2%
Total Carbohydrate	10.6g	4%
Dietary Fiber	2.3g	8%
Total Sugars	6.9g	
Protein	0.9g	

Tips: Popsicles last for 6-8 months in the freezer if kept at a constant temperature.

APPLE CHIA PARFAITS

Prep time: 10 min	Cook time: 00 min	Servings: 6

Ingredients

- 1/2 cup chia seeds
- 2 cups coconut milk
- 2 tsp vanilla extract

Caramel Apple Ingredients

- 1 tbsp coconut oil
- 3 granny smith apples, cored and roughly chopped
- 1 cup coconut sugar
- 3/4 cup coconut milk
- 1/2 tsp cinnamon
- pinch of salt

214

Instructions

- Combine the chia seeds, coconut milk and vanilla extract in a small bowl. Cover and refrigerate to soak for at least 2 hours, ideally overnight.
- To make the caramel apples, melt the coconut oil in a saucepan and add the apples.
- Fry the apples for a few minutes, then add the coconut sugar and coconut milk.
- Cook until a thick caramel form (stirring constantly) and the apples soften.
- Add cinnamon and salt, then stir to combine.
- Garnish the chia pudding with caramel apples and serve.

NUTRITION FACTS (PER SERVING)

Calories	299	
Total Fat	29.7g	38%
Saturated Fat	25.5g	127%
Cholesterol	0mg	0%
Sodium	19mg	1%
Total Carbohydrate	8.4g	3%
Dietary Fiber	3.9g	14%
Total Sugars	4.3g	
Protein	3.3g	

Tips: chia seeds are full of important nutrients. They are an excellent source of omega-3 fatty acids, rich in antioxidants, and they provide fiber, iron, and calcium. Omega-3 fatty acids help raise HDL cholesterol, the "good" cholesterol that protects against heart attack and stroke.

LEMON POPPY SEED MUFFINS

Prep time: 10 min	Cook time: 20 min	Servings: 12

Ingredients

- *4 L size eggs*
- *1/3 cup lemon juice*
- *zest of one lemon (minced)*
- *1/3 cup + 1 tbsp maple syrup*
- *1/4 cup coconut oil (melted)*
- *1 tsp pure vanilla extract*
- *1/2 tsp pure almond extract*
- *2 cups blanched almond flour*
- *1/3 cup tapioca flour*
- *3/4 tsp baking soda*
- *1/4 tsp salt*
- *2 tbsp poppy seeds*

Instructions

- Preheat your oven to 350 degrees F and line a 12-muffin pan with parchment paper.
- In a medium bowl, mix the almond flour, tapioca flour, baking powder and salt.
- In a large bowl, whisk the eggs, lemon juice, lemon zest, maple syrup, coconut oil and both extracts together until combined. Gently stir the dry mixture into the wet mixture until just combined, then add the poppy seeds to distribute them evenly.
- Divide muffin batter evenly between ramekins and 3/4 fill to make 12 muffins.
- Bake in preheated oven for about 16 to 18 minutes or until center is firm and arched and a toothpick comes out clean in center.
- Leave muffins to cool on wire racks while basting. Mix the melted coconut butter and honey and drizzle the muffins. It becomes difficult when it cools.

NUTRITION FACTS (PER SERVING)

Calories	202	
Total Fat	14.1g	18%
Saturated Fat	5g	25%
Cholesterol	0mg	0%
Sodium	151mg	7%
Total Carbohydrate	13g	5%
Dietary Fiber	2.2g	8%
Total Sugars	5.7g	
Protein	5.5g	

Tips: You can store leftovers in the refrigerator for 3 days.

PUMPKIN BARS WITH HONEY FROSTING

Prep time: 15 min	Cook time: 35 min	Servings: 12

Ingredients

- 2 cups almond flour
- 1/2 tsp salt
- 1/2 tsp baking soda
- ¼ tsp baking powder
- 2 tsp pumpkin pie spice
- 1/4 cup almond butter
- 2 tbsp coconut oil
- 1/4 cup coconut sugar
- 2 tbsp maple syrup
- 2 tsp vanilla extract
- 2 tbsp almond milk
- 1 cup pumpkin puree

Honey frosting:

- *1/2 cup coconut oil*
- *1/3 cup honey*
- *1/4 tsp cinnamon*
- *1 1/4 tbsp coconut flour*
- *2 1/2 tbsp coconut milk*
- *1 tbsp coconut sugar*

Instructions

- To prepare the bars, preheat the oven to 350 degrees. Grease, line and reserve an 8x8 baking dish.
- Combine almond flour, salt, baking powder, baking powder and pumpkin pie seasoning in a small bowl and mix well. Put aside.
- In a medium to large microwave safe bowl, add coconut oil and almond butter. Cook in the microwave and heat for 30 seconds. Stir well and return to microwave to heat completely. Remove from microwave and stir until well combined.
- Add the coconut sugar, maple syrup, vanilla and almond milk to the almond butter and coconut oil and stir until combined. Add the pumpkin puree and mix well.
- Add the dry ingredients to the wet ingredients and mix well until all the ingredients are combined.
- Pour the mixture into the prepared pan and place in the oven for 30 to 35 minutes, until the center is set. The bars are slightly damp. Let them cool in the pan for 15 minutes, then place the bars in the refrigerator for at least 30 minutes or up to a few days.

- While the bars are cooling, make the frosting. In a medium bowl, whisk butter or ghee for about 1 minute until smooth and creamy.
- Add maple syrup, cinnamon, coconut flour, coconut milk and coconut sugar and beat until combined, about 2 minutes. If you are using ghee, add an extra tablespoon of coconut flour.
- When the bars are completely cold, take them out of the pan and cover them with the frosting. Chill for another 15 minutes in the refrigerator. Cut and enjoy!

NUTRITION FACTS (PER SERVING)		
Calories	168	
Total Fat	12.5g	16%
Saturated Fat	3.2g	16%
Cholesterol	0mg	0%
Sodium	151mg	7%
Total Carbohydrate	12.4g	5%
Dietary Fiber	2.7g	10%
Total Sugars	7.5g	
Protein	4.4g	

Tips: store these bars in the fridge for up to a week or in the freezer for a month.

5. SMOOTHIES AND DRINKS

APPLE PIE SMOOTHIE

Prep time: 10 min	Cook time: 0 min	Servings: 1

Ingredients

- 1 frozen banana, small
- 2/3 cup apple sauce, unsweetened
- 1 teaspoon cinnamon
- 1 teaspoon vanilla extract
- 1/2 cup coconut milk, unsweetened

Instructions

- Place all ingredients in a high-speed blender.
- Blend until smooth.

NUTRITION FACTS (PER SERVING)

Calories	186	
Total Fat	4.9g	6%
Saturated Fat	4.1g	21%
Cholesterol	0mg	0%
Sodium	2mg	0%
Total Carbohydrate	35.5g	13%
Dietary Fiber	5.5g	20%
Total Sugars	20.3g	
Protein	1.2g	

Tips: Use any plant-based milk as a substitute of coconut milk.

CILANTRO PEAR GREEN SMOOTHIE

Prep time: 10 min	Cook time: 0 min	Servings: 1

Ingredients

- *1/4 of a small bunch of fresh cilantros*
- *1/8 avocado*
- *1/4 small pear*
- *1/4 small apple*
- *1 small bananas*
- *1 cup water*
- *1 cup ice (200g)*

Instructions

- Place all ingredients in a high-speed blender.
- Blend until smooth.

NUTRITION FACTS (PER SERVING)

Calories	193	
Total Fat	5.4g	7%
Saturated Fat	1.1g	6%
Cholesterol	0mg	0%
Sodium	17mg	1%
Total Carbohydrate	38.7g	14%
Dietary Fiber	7g	25%
Total Sugars	21.9g	
Protein	2.1g	

Tips: Green smoothies are a great way to get my daily recommended serving of fruits and veggies.

STRAWBERRY-KIWI SMOOTHIE

Prep time: 10 min	Cook time: 0 min	Servings: 1

Ingredients

- 1/2 cup frozen strawberries, roughly chopped
- 1/2 cup frozen kiwi, roughly chopped
- 2 fresh mint leaves
- 1 cup coconut milk
- 2 cups crushed ice

Instructions

- Place all ingredients in a high-speed blender.
- Blend until smooth.

NUTRITION FACTS (PER SERVING)

Calories	130	
Total Fat	4.7g	6%
Saturated Fat	4g	20%
Cholesterol	0mg	0%
Sodium	7mg	0%
Total Carbohydrate	22.4g	8%
Dietary Fiber	6.1g	22%
Total Sugars	12.5g	
Protein	1.8g	

Tips: A strawberry and banana smoothie is good for you because strawberries are rich in fiber, vitamins and antioxidants. They are among the top 20 most antioxidant-rich fruits. One serving of strawberries (about 8 berries) contains more vitamin C than an orange.

PINA COLADA SMOOTHIE

Prep time: 10 min	Cook time: 0 min	Servings: 2

Ingredients

- 2 cups fresh pineapple (diced)
- 4 tbsp coconut flakes
- 1/4 cup coconut milk
- 1/4 cup water
- 1/2 tbsp lime juice
- 1/2 tsp honey

- *1/2 cup ice cubes (optional)*

Instructions

- Place all ingredients in a high-speed blender.
- Blend until smooth.

NUTRITION FACTS (PER SERVING)		
Calories	191	
Total Fat	7.6g	10%
Saturated Fat	7g	35%
Cholesterol	0mg	0%
Sodium	9mg	0%
Total Carbohydrate	33.3g	12%
Dietary Fiber	4.4g	16%
Total Sugars	21.6g	
Protein	1.4g	

Tips: Eating a few slices of fresh pineapple a day can defend your body from harmful free radicals and disease, help your digestion by cleaning the body's organs and blood, increase your energy intake and boost metabolism, nourish your hair, skin, nails and teeth and keep you generally healthy

CANTALOUPE SMOOTHIE

Prep time: 10 min	Cook time: 0 min	Servings: 1

Ingredients

- *1/2 cantaloupe*
- *1 cup coconut milk*
- *1 1/2 cups ice*

Instructions

- Place all ingredients in a high-speed blender.
- Blend until smooth.

NUTRITION FACTS (PER SERVING)

Calories	212	
Total Fat	20.1g	26%
Saturated Fat	18g	90%
Cholesterol	0mg	0%
Sodium	61mg	3%
Total Carbohydrate	8.8g	3%
Dietary Fiber	0.3g	1%
Total Sugars	4.7g	
Protein	1.3g	

Tips: Cantaloupe contains several ingredients - fiber, potassium, and vitamin C - that contribute to keeping our heart healthy. Food high in fiber help control blood pressure and lower LDL and the bad cholesterol.

BLUEBERRY BLAST SMOOTHIE

| Prep time: 10 min | Cook time: 0 min | Servings: 1 |

Ingredients

- 1 frozen banana
- 1/2 cup blueberries
- 1 tbsp almond butter
- 1 unsweetened almond milk

Instructions

- Place all ingredients in a high-speed blender.
- Blend until smooth.

NUTRITION FACTS (PER SERVING)

Calories	231	
Total Fat	9.6g	12%
Saturated Fat	0.8g	4%
Cholesterol	0mg	0%
Sodium	12mg	1%
Total Carbohydrate	36.6g	13%
Dietary Fiber	6g	21%
Total Sugars	20.3g	
Protein	5.1g	

Tips: According to a few studies, a bowl of blueberries can help in boosting immunity and can reduce the risk of diabetes, obesity and heart diseases.

MINT AND CITRUS DRINK

Prep time: 10 min	Cook time: 0 min	Servings: 4

Ingredients

- *1 lemon, sliced*
- *2 limes, sliced*
- *1/4 cup fresh lemon juice*
- *1/4 cup fresh mint leaves*
- *2 liters water*
- *1 cup ice*

Instructions

- For the lemon juice at the bottom of a jug.

- Add the lemon wedges, limes and mint leaves.
- Pour in the water and stir everything well.
- Add ice and serve immediately, or store ice and refrigerate until ready to serve.

NUTRITION FACTS (PER SERVING)

Calories	20	
Total Fat	0.3g	0%
Saturated Fat	0.2g	1%
Cholesterol	0mg	0%
Sodium	21mg	1%
Total Carbohydrate	5.7g	2%
Dietary Fiber	1.8g	6%
Total Sugars	1.3g	
Protein	0.7g	

Tips: This drink is great for cleansing your body. One of the major benefits in drinking lemon water is that it aids in weight loss and gives your body natural electrolytes.

GINGER TURMERIC ORANGE JUICE

Prep time: 10 min	Cook time: 0 min	Servings: 4

Ingredients

- 2 apples, peeled and chopped
- 4 oranges, peeled
- 1 lemon, peeled
- 1 tbsp fresh ginger, minced
- 1 tbsp fresh turmeric, minced
- 2 cups water

Instructions

- Put the apples, oranges and lemon in a blender and mix until smooth.

- Add the ginger and turmeric and give it another boost.
- Pour in the water and squeeze until you get a smooth juice.
- Add more water for a milder juice.

NUTRITION FACTS (PER SERVING)

Calories	159	
Total Fat	0.7g	1%
Saturated Fat	0.1g	1%
Cholesterol	0mg	0%
Sodium	6mg	0%
Total Carbohydrate	40.4g	15%
Dietary Fiber	8.1g	29%
Total Sugars	29.3g	
Protein	2.4g	

Tips: Studies suggest 500–2,000 mg of turmeric per day has potential benefits. Turmeric in extract form performs the best.

GREEN SMOOTHIE

Prep time: 10 min	Cook time: 0 min	Servings: 2

Ingredients

- 1/4 cup grapes
- 1/4 orange, peeled
- 1/4 apple, quartered, seeded
- 1/8 cup fresh pineapple chunks
- 1small banana
- 1 small carrot, peeled and halved
- 1/2 cups fresh spinach

Instructions

- Place all ingredients in a high-speed blender.
- Blend until smooth.

NUTRITION FACTS (PER SERVING)

Calories	100	
Total Fat	0.4g	1%
Saturated Fat	0.1g	0%
Cholesterol	0mg	0%
Sodium	40mg	2%
Total Carbohydrate	25.2g	9%
Dietary Fiber	4.2g	15%
Total Sugars	16.2g	
Protein	1.5g	

Tips: Simply prepare your entire days' or even several days' worth of green smoothies in the morning and pack it up to take with you. Keep it refrigerated as much as possible.

BANANA CHAI SMOOTHIE

Prep time: 10 min	Cook time: 0 min	Servings: 1

Ingredients

- *1 frozen banana*
- *1 tablespoons coconut milk*
- *1/4 teaspoon each of vanilla*
- *1/4 teaspoon cloves*
- *1/4 teaspoon ginger*
- *1/4 teaspoon cinnamon*
- *1 cup of water*

Instructions

- Place all ingredients in a high-speed blender.
- Blend until smooth.

NUTRITION FACTS (PER SERVING)

Calories	132	
Total Fat	4.1g	5%
Saturated Fat	3.3g	17%
Cholesterol	0mg	0%
Sodium	12mg	1%
Total Carbohydrate	25.1g	9%
Dietary Fiber	3.5g	13%
Total Sugars	13g	
Protein	1.5g	

Tips: Chia seeds contain large amounts of fiber and omega-3 fatty acids, plenty of high-quality protein, and several essential minerals and antioxidants. They may improve digestive health, blood levels of heart-healthy omega-3s, and risk factors for heart disease and diabetes

TROPICAL SMOOTHIE

Prep time: 10 min	Cook time: 0 min	Servings: 2

Ingredients

- 1/4 pineapple, peeled and cubed
- 1 medium apple, cored and cubed
- 1 banana, sliced
- 1/2 tsp chia seed
- 1 cup unsweetened coconut milk
- 1 tbsp 100% MCT oil

Instructions

- Place all ingredients in a high-speed blender.
- Blend until smooth.

NUTRITION FACTS (PER SERVING)

Calories	202	
Total Fat	10g	13%
Saturated Fat	9.1g	46%
Cholesterol	0mg	0%
Sodium	2mg	0%
Total Carbohydrate	33.3g	12%
Dietary Fiber	5.6g	20%
Total Sugars	20.9g	
Protein	1.3g	

Tips: Pineapples are loaded with antioxidants and omega 3 fatty acids. It helps to fight ageing, reduces acne scars and keeps skin beautiful and healthy.

MANGO GREEN SMOOTHIE

Prep time: 10 min	Cook time: 0 min	Servings: 2

Ingredients

- 2 oranges, peeled
- 2 cups pineapple, chopped
- 6 kale leaves, stalks removed
- 2 cups mango
- 2 cups water

Instructions

- Place all ingredients in a high-speed blender.
- Blend until smooth.

NUTRITION FACTS (PER SERVING)

Calories	568	
Total Fat	2.1g	3%
Saturated Fat	0.4g	2%
Cholesterol	0mg	0%
Sodium	51mg	2%
Total Carbohydrate	143g	52%
Dietary Fiber	19.7g	70%
Total Sugars	112g	
Protein	10g	

Tips: mango flesh contains prebiotic dietary fiber, which helps feed good bacteria in the gut.

CHAI TEA SMOOTHIE

Prep time: 10 min	Cook time: 0 min	Servings: 2

Ingredients

- 1 cup unsweetened coconut
- 1 chai tea bag
- 1 very ripe frozen banana, cut into chunks
- 1/4 teaspoon pure vanilla extract

Instructions

- In a small saucepan on the stovetop, heat the milk in for a minute or two, until hot and starting to boil.
- Put the tea bag in the milk and put it in the refrigerator until it cools.
- Combine the tea infused milk, banana and vanilla in a blender and blend until smooth.

NUTRITION FACTS (PER SERVING)

Calories	108	
Total Fat	0.4g	1%
Saturated Fat	0.1g	1%
Cholesterol	0mg	0%
Sodium	1mg	0%
Total Carbohydrate	27.1g	10%
Dietary Fiber	3.1g	11%
Total Sugars	14.6g	
Protein	1.3g	

Tips: While they make a fantastic healthy breakfast or snack throughout the day, smoothies are not a good idea before bedtime.

COCONUT STRAWBERRY DRINK

Prep time: 10 min	Cook time: 0 min	Servings: 2

Ingredients

- *8 oz. coconut water*
- *1/4 cup fresh lime or lemon juice*
- *12 oz. frozen strawberries*
- *8 oz. crushed ice*

Instructions

- Place all ingredients in a high-speed blender.
- Blend until smooth.

NUTRITION FACTS (PER SERVING)

Calories	85	
Total Fat	0.5g	1%
Saturated Fat	0.4g	2%
Cholesterol	0mg	0%
Sodium	125mg	5%
Total Carbohydrate	19.5g	7%
Dietary Fiber	4.8g	17%
Total Sugars	13.6g	
Protein	1.1g	

Tips: With only 45 calories in a cup, coconut water is a great substitute for higher calorie drinks like sodas or juice.

COCONUT MILK HOT CHOCOLATE

Prep time: 10 min	Cook time: 0 min	Servings: 2

Ingredients

- *1 can full fat coconut milk*
- *1.5 oz good quality dark chocolate, finely chopped*
- *1/4 tsp vanilla extract*

Instructions

- Heat the coconut milk in a saucepan over medium heat until hot but not boiling.
- Add chocolate and vanilla extract and stir until completely melted.
- Serve hot.

NUTRITION FACTS (PER SERVING)

Calories	164	
Total Fat	12.7g	16%
Saturated Fat	10.1g	51%
Cholesterol	2mg	1%
Sodium	10mg	0%
Total Carbohydrate	13.4g	5%
Dietary Fiber	1.5g	5%
Total Sugars	10.3g	
Protein	2g	

Tips: chocolate milk provides eight essential nutrients, including calcium, vitamin D and potassium, as well as protein, vitamins A and B12, riboflavin and phosphorus.

AVOCADO BLUEBERRY SMOOTHIE

Prep time: 10 min	Cook time: 0 min	Servings: 2

Ingredients

- *1 cup frozen blueberry*
- *1 ripe avocado, roughly chopped*
- *1 tbsp cocoa powder*
- *1 1/2 cup coconut milk*
- *1/2 tsp vanilla*
- *1 tbsp maple syrup*
- *dark chocolate, grated*

Instructions

- Place all ingredients in a high-speed blender.
- Blend until smooth.

NUTRITION FACTS (PER SERVING)

Calories	321	
Total Fat	23.5g	30%
Saturated Fat	7.1g	35%
Cholesterol	1mg	0%
Sodium	11mg	0%
Total Carbohydrate	29.5g	11%
Dietary Fiber	10.2g	37%
Total Sugars	15g	
Protein	3g	

Tips: According to a few studies, a bowl of blueberries can help in boosting immunity and can reduce the risk of diabetes, obesity and heart diseases. Moreover, consuming a small portion of berries daily can help in strengthening the metabolism and prevent any kind of metabolic syndrome and deficiency.

MATCHA SMOOTHIE

Prep time: 10 min	Cook time: 0 min	Servings: 2

Ingredients

- 2 bananas
- 1 avocado
- 1/4 cup matcha powder
- 3 cups baby kale
- 2 cups coconut milk
- ice (optional)

Instructions

- Place all ingredients in a high-speed blender.
- Blend until smooth.

254

NUTRITION FACTS (PER SERVING)

Calories	472	
Total Fat	32.4g	41%
Saturated Fat	14.2g	71%
Cholesterol	0mg	0%
Sodium	73mg	3%
Total Carbohydrate	45.8g	17%
Dietary Fiber	11.6g	41%
Total Sugars	15.1g	
Protein	6.9g	

Tips: Matcha is high in a catechin called EGCG. According to research, it might have cancer-fighting effects on the body.

PUMPKIN BANANA SMOOTHIE

Prep time: 10 min	Cook time: 0 min	Servings: 2

Ingredients

- 3/4 cups unsweetened almond milk
- 1 cup crushed ice
- 1/2 frozen banana
- 1 tsp finely ground flaxseed
- 1/3 cup pumpkin puree
- 1 tbsp honey
- 1/4 tsp cinnamon
- 1/4 tsp nutmeg
- 1/4 tsp ginger

Instructions

- Place all ingredients in a high-speed blender.
- Blend until smooth.

NUTRITION FACTS (PER SERVING)

Calories   192
Total Fat 4g   5%
Saturated Fat 0.7g   3%
Cholesterol 0mg   0%
Sodium 141mg   6%
Total Carbohydrate 40.6g   15%
Dietary Fiber 5.8g   21%
Total Sugars 27.4g
Protein 2.9g

Tips: Bananas are one of the most popular fruits in the world. They're full important nutrients, but eating too many could end up doing more harm than good.

AVOCADO GREEN SMOOTHIE

Prep time: 10 min	Cook time: 0 min	Servings: 2

Ingredients

- 1 avocado
- 1 cup fresh baby kale
- 1/2 cucumber, sliced
- 1 cup unsweetened almond milk
- 1 leek stalk, roughly chopped
- 1/4 cup water or 1-2 ice cubes
- 1 tbsp fresh lemon juice
- 1/4 tsp turmeric
- 2 tbsp melted coconut oil

Instructions

- Place all ingredients in a high-speed blender.
- Blend until smooth.

NUTRITION FACTS (PER SERVING)

Calories	336	
Total Fat	30.5g	39%
Saturated Fat	7.9g	39%
Cholesterol	0mg	0%
Sodium	200mg	9%
Total Carbohydrate	16.2g	6%
Dietary Fiber	8.2g	29%
Total Sugars	1.9g	
Protein	4g	

Tips: kale is loaded with powerful antioxidants like quercetin and kaempferol.

RED VELVET SMOOTHIE

Prep time: 10 min	Cook time: 0 min	Servings: 2

Ingredients

- 1 beet
- 1/2 banana
- 1 tsp carob powder
- 1 cup full-fat coconut milk
- crushed ice

Instructions

- Place all ingredients in a high-speed blender.
- Blend until smooth.

NUTRITION FACTS (PER SERVING)

Calories	334	
Total Fat	29.4g	38%
Saturated Fat	25.9g	130%
Cholesterol	0mg	0%
Sodium	59mg	3%
Total Carbohydrate	19.4g	7%
Dietary Fiber	4.5g	16%
Total Sugars	12.2g	
Protein	4.1g	

Tips: Beetroots contain a lot of nutrients. They are a great source of fiber, vitamin B9, potassium, iron, and vitamin C. They are associated with numerous health benefits, such as improved blood flow, lower blood pressure, and increased exercise performance.

SPICY TOMATO SMOOTHIE

Prep time: 10 min	Cook time: 0 min	Servings: 2

Ingredients

- *1/2 cup chopped tomato*
- *1/4 cup chopped cucumber*
- *1/2 avocado*
- *1/3 cup frozen spinach*
- *1 teaspoon black pepper*
- *squeeze of lemon*
- *1/2 cup ice*

Instructions

- Place all ingredients in a high-speed blender.
- Blend until smooth.

NUTRITION FACTS (PER SERVING)

Calories	246	
Total Fat	20.1g	26%
Saturated Fat	4.2g	21%
Cholesterol	0mg	0%
Sodium	24mg	1%
Total Carbohydrate	19g	7%
Dietary Fiber	8.9g	32%
Total Sugars	9.1g	
Protein	3.6g	

Tips: Tomatoes are the major dietary source of the antioxidant lycopene, which has been linked to many health benefits, including reduced risk of heart disease and cancer. They are also a great source of vitamin C, potassium, folate, and vitamin K.

GREEN CLEANSING SMOOTHIE

Prep time: 10 min	Cook time: 0 min	Servings: 2

Ingredients

- 1/2 cup of water
- 1 cup fresh spinach leaves
- 1 kiwi
- 1/2-inch fresh ginger, peeled and minced
- 1 tablespoon fresh lime juice
- 1 green apple

Instructions

- Place all ingredients in a high-speed blender.

- Blend until smooth.

NUTRITION FACTS (PER SERVING)

Calories	183	
Total Fat	1g	1%
Saturated Fat	0.1g	0%
Cholesterol	0mg	0%
Sodium	33mg	1%
Total Carbohydrate	47.4g	17%
Dietary Fiber	8.7g	31%
Total Sugars	30.9g	
Protein	2.6g	

Tips: Spinach is a superfood. It is loaded with tons of nutrients in a low-calorie package. Dark, leafy greens like spinach are important for skin, hair, and bone health. They also provide protein, iron, vitamins, and minerals.

MINTY MORNING GREEN SMOOTHIE

Prep time: 10 min	Cook time: 0 min	Servings: 2

Ingredients

- *1/2 frozen banana*
- *1/2 small avocado*
- *1 cup of baby spinach*
- *1/2 raw cucumber*
- *1/2 cup coconut milk*
- *1/2 cup water*
- *1 tbsp fresh mint*
- *1/2 squeezed lemon juice*
- *1 tbsp maple syrup*

Instructions

- Place all ingredients in a high-speed blender.
- Blend until smooth.

NUTRITION FACTS (PER SERVING)

Calories	414	
Total Fat	29.2g	37%
Saturated Fat	25.5g	128%
Cholesterol	0mg	0%
Sodium	52mg	2%
Total Carbohydrate	41.1g	15%
Dietary Fiber	6g	21%
Total Sugars	26.5g	
Protein	5.5g	

Tips: Cucumbers contain magnesium, potassium, and vitamin K. These 3 nutrients are vital for the proper functioning of the cardiovascular system.

BLUEBERRY ACAI SMOOTHIE

Prep time: 10 min	Cook time: 0 min	Servings: 2

Ingredients

- 1 cup coconut milk
- 1 1/2 frozen bananas
- 1 cup frozen blueberries
- 1 cup frozen strawberries
- 1 cup acai juice
- 3/4 cup ice

Instructions

- Place all ingredients in a high-speed blender.
- Blend until smooth.

NUTRITION FACTS (PER SERVING)

Calories	240	
Total Fat	7.2g	9%
Saturated Fat	5.2g	26%
Cholesterol	0mg	0%
Sodium	18mg	1%
Total Carbohydrate	44.7g	16%
Dietary Fiber	6.8g	24%
Total Sugars	23.2g	
Protein	2.7g	

Tips: Acai berries have a unique nutritional profile for a fruit, as they're somewhat high in fat and low in sugar.

WATERMELON & LIME FRAPPÉ

Prep time: 10 min	Cook time: 0 min	Servings: 2

Ingredients

- 3 cups chopped watermelon
- 1 lime, juice only
- 1 tsp maple syrup
- 1 cup crushed ice or ice cubes

Instructions

- Place all ingredients in a high-speed blender.
- Blend until smooth.

NUTRITION FACTS (PER SERVING)

Calories	87	
Total Fat	0.4g	0%
Saturated Fat	0.2g	1%
Cholesterol	0mg	0%
Sodium	8mg	0%
Total Carbohydrate	22.9g	8%
Dietary Fiber	1.8g	7%
Total Sugars	16.6g	
Protein	1.6g	

Tips: Watermelon is rich in an amino acid called citrulline that may help move blood through your body and can lower your blood pressure. Your heart also enjoys the perks of all the lycopene watermelon contains

4 WEEKS DIET PLAN

TIPS AND TRICKS

Below you fill wind of a four-week diet plan. You can find the recipes for each of the dishes, listed in the diet plan, among the recipes in this book. The four-week diet plan will help you plan your meals ahead and lose your excess weight easily.

Tips:

- If you wish to lose weight rapidly, you can skip the dessert part of the daily meal plan.
- For best results, you should exercise. We prepared an exercise plan for you to practice.
- If you feel hungry throughout the day, you can always snack on raw fruit or vegetables. For example, green apples, fresh celery or baby carrots can make for a great snack. You can also eat 10 pieces of nuts when hungry, it will keep you full and fill you with energy.
- If you feel you need more energy, you can always add extra veggies (or extra eggs) to your breakfast, lunch or dinner plates or extra pieces of fruit to your smoothies.
- You can play with the smoothies – if you do not fancy a suggested smoothie, you can always substitute it with something you like, from the recipe section.
- It is best to buy the ingredients for your meals a week ahead. This way, you will be well organized and won't be tempted to buy other food and your food will still stay fresh enough if you store it correctly.

1ST WEEK MEAL PLAN

Day	Breakfast	Snack	Lunch	Dinner	Dessert
1	Apple Pie Smoothie	Avocado Fries	Tarragon-Lemon Roasted Turkey Breast with Cooked Vegetables by Choice	Carrot Soup	Fudge
2	Mushroom Omelette	Tortilla Chips	Orange and Pork Stir-Fry, Fresh Vegetable Salat By Choice	Salmon with Toasted Garlic and Broccoli	Coconut Date Balls
3	Roasted Spiced Cauliflower	Fresh Fruit by Choice, 1 Piece	Beef Stuffed Bell Peppers	Baked Mustard Chicken	Pumpkin Bars with Honey Frosting
4	Matcha Smoothie	Cabbage Chips	Chicken Stew	Roasted Red Pepper and Tomato Soup	Sweet Potato Brownies
5	Strawberry Pancakes	Fresh Fruit by Choice, 2 Pieces	Mushroom Lamb Stew	Cauliflower and Spinach Soup	Coconut Milk Custard
6	Fish Sticks	Fresh Fruit by Choice, 1 Piece	Green Cleansing Smoothie	Trout, Avocado and Egg Salad	Chocolate Fat Bombs
7	Smoked Tuna, Avocado, Devilled Eggs	Carrot Fries	Tomato and Pork Soup	Pulled Chicken Stuffed Squash	Fried Banana

2ND WEEK MEAL PLAN

Day	Breakfast	Snack	Lunch	Dinner	Dessert
1	Blueberry Blast Smoothie	Avocado Fries	Tuna with Veggies in Teriyaki-Style	Honey Garlic Turkey and Vegetables	Dried Fruit Bars
2	Mango Green Smoothie	Tortilla Chips	Beef with Spinach, Sweet Potatoes and Mushrooms	Seafood Chowder	Blueberry Cobbler
3	Pina Colada Smoothie	Fresh Fruit by Choice, 1 Piece	Trout, Avocado and Egg Salad	Tomato and Pork Soup	Apple Pie Muffins
4	Overnight Oats Grain Free	Cabbage Chips	Salmon with Mangos	Carrot Soup	Almond Tapioca Pudding
5	Avocado Green Smoothie	Fresh Fruit by Choice, 2 Pieces	Ground Pork and Zucchini Stir-Fry	Chicken Breast and Apple Skillet	Pecans and Coconut Macaroons
6	Mango Green Smoothie	Fresh Fruit by Choice, 1 Piece	Sautéed Turkey and Cabbage	Baked Mustard Chicken with Fresh Veggies	Apple Chia Parfaits
7	Minty Morning Green Smoothie	Carrot Fries	Beef Stuffed Bell Peppers	Turkey Salad with Balsamic	Flourless Chocolate Cakes

3RD WEEK MEAL PLAN

Day	Breakfast	Snacks	Lunch	Dinner	Dessert
1	Coconut Granola	Fresh Fruit by Choice, 1 Piece	Asian Turkey Cabbage Salad	Strawberry-Kiwi Smoothie	Lemon Poppy Seed Muffins
2	Strawberry Donuts	Avocado Fries	Seafood Chowder	Mushroom Lamb Stew	Sweet Potato Brownies
3	Blueberry Blast Smoothie	Fresh Fruit by Choice, 1 Piece	Turkey Wings	Spicy Tomato Smoothie	Chocolate Oranges
4	Ginger Turmeric Orange Juice	Cabbage Chips	Salmon with Toasted Garlic Broccoli	Turkey Salad with Balsamic	Banana Apricots Cookies
5	Fried Zucchini with Cool Mint Dip	Fresh Fruit by Choice, 1 Pieces	Cauliflower and Spinach Soup	Lemon-Rosemary Seared Trout	Chocolate Almond Balls
6	Parsnips Strips, Fresh Carrots (2 pieces)	Fresh Fruit by Choice, 1 Piece	Ground Pork and Zucchini Stir-Fry	Chicken Stew	Dried Fruit Bars
7	Avocado Fries	100 g Fresh Vegetables, Sliced	Salmon with Mango	Ground Pork and Zucchini Stir-Fry	Banana Apricots Cookies

4TH WEEK MEAL PLAN

Day	Breakfast	Snacks	Lunch	Dinner	Dessert
1	Chai Tea Smoothie	Parsnips Strips	Sautéed Turkey and Cabbage	Beef Stuffed Bell Peppers	Banana Bread
2	Kale Omelette	Fresh Fruit by Choice, 2 Pieces	Orange and Pork Stir-Fry	Seafood Chowder	Dried Fruit Bars
3	Coconut Strawberry Drink	Carrot Fries	Honey Garlic Turkey and Vegetables	Lemon-Rosemary Seared Trout	Pumpkin Bars with Honey Frosting
4	Turkey Stuffed Avocado	Fresh Fruit by Choice, 2 Pieces	Pulled Chicken Stuffed Squash	Beef and Vegetable Soup	Almond Tapioca Pudding
5	Green Smoothie	Avocado Fries	Chicken Kale, And Broccoli Soup	Baked Mustard Chicken	Fruit Cake
6	Buffalo Lamb Meatballs	Fresh Fruit by Choice, 1 Piece	Asian Turkey Cabbage Salad.	Salmon with Toasted Garlic Broccoli	Chocolate Pudding
7	Green Cleansing Smoothie	Tortilla Chips	Sautéed Turkey and Cabbage	Tuna with Veggies in Teriyaki-Style	Chocolate Fat Bombs

4 WEEKS EXERCISE PLAN

ENDOMORPH DIET AND EXERCISE

Exercising is very important for any endomorph as it will help speed up metabolism. Since endomorphs have higher percentage of body fat and lower percentage of muscle tissue in their bodies, regular exercising activity can change this ration in an endomorph favor and thus, shape their body.

So how much exercising is actually needed to lose as much fat tissue as possible? A lot. In order to stimulate a slow metabolism, the endomorph should use every free moment to move.

It would be ideal if an endomorph would exercise twice a day, every day of the week. It is advisable that endomorphs do aerobic activities (cardio training) in the morning, for around 30-40 minutes, and then later in the day, a 30- or 40-minute training with weights (power training).

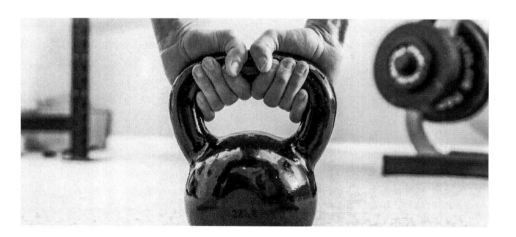

Ideally, an endomorph should train with high intensity: moderate to high loads, fast movements and short breaks between sets of exercises (one- or 2-min breaks). The goal is to accelerate the heart rate and breathing throughout the workout or in other words – to sweat like crazy.

Training twice a day is of course not possible for a majority of people, due to their busy work and family responsibilities throughout the day.

The second-best option is that endomorphs exercise once a day, but combine training with weights and aerobic training. First, 20 minutes of training with weights and doing exercises for power, followed by a 20- 40 minutes aerobic training (running, cycling, swimming, etc.). Since endomorphs usually have very good regeneration process, it is advisable to only take a rest day once or twice a week.

It might not be the healthiest option if a previously inactive person will suddenly start a though twice-a-day training regime of physical activity. It is better that the principle of gradualness is observed – start with a little exercise and then gradually increase the intensity and length of exercises.

The general advise for any endomorph would be: move as much as you can! Endomorphs should use every possible moment to move around. You can cycle to work, walk whenever possible, use stairs instead of a lift or move around the house instead of sitting in front of TV. Do some gardening and cleaning or wash your car on a lazy Sunday. These are just a few ideas for an active lifestyle so be creative! Every movement is better than none. The more, the better!

In the following pages, you can find a 4-week workout plan for an endomorph. Time and intensity of individual exercise will increase gradually over days and weeks. If you find it to thought, you can reduce the number of repetitions or add a few minutes of pause. If you find it too easy, add some more exercises by choice or double the repetitions! Make sure to warm up well prior to exercising and stretching well after the exercises, to avoid potential injury and sour muscles.

1ST WEEK EXERCISE PLAN

MONDAY	• 20 squats, 1 min rest, repeat 2x • 30 sec plank, 1 min rest, repeat 2x • 20 crunches, 1 min rest, repeat 3x • 20 lunges, 1 min rest, repeat 2x • 30 sec walls sit, 1 min rest, repeat 2x • 10 pushups, 1 min rest, repeat 2x • 10 1-pound weights lift, repeat 2x each hand • Run fast 2 min, walk 2 min, repeat 5x
TUSEDAY	**REST DAY**
WEDNESDAY	• 20 squats, 1 min rest, repeat 2x • 30 sec plank, 1 min rest, repeat 2x • 20 crunches, 1 min rest, repeat 4x • 20 lunges, 1 min rest, repeat 2x • 10 pushups, 1 min rest, repeat 2x • Jogging with high knees for 2 min • 10 1-pound weights lift, repeat 4x each hand • 10 hip raises, 1 min rest, repeat 2x each side • Jogging with high knees for 4 min • Run fast 2 min, walk 2 min, repeat 6x
THURSTDAY	• 25 squats, 1 min rest, repeat 2x • 35 sec plank, 1 min rest, repeat 2x • 20 crunches, 1 min rest, repeat 3x • 20 lunges, 1 min rest, repeat 2x • 35 sec walls sit, 1 min rest, repeat 2x • 10 pushups, 1 min rest, repeat 2x • 10 1-pound weights lift, repeat 2x each hand • Run for 20 min
FRIDAY	**REST DAY**
SATHURDAY	• 20 squats, 1 min rest, repeat 2x • 35 sec plank, 1 min rest, repeat 2x • 20 crunches, 1 min rest, repeat 3x • 20 lunges, 1 min rest, repeat 2x • 35 sec walls sit, 1 min rest, repeat 2x • 10 pushups, 1 min rest, repeat 2x • 20 sit ups, 1 min rest, repeat 2x • 10x reverse lunge, 1 min rest, repeat 2x • 10 mountain climbers, 1 min rest, repeat 2x • 10 1-pound weights lift, 30 sec rest, repeat 4x each hand • Jogging with high knees for 2 min • Run fast 2 min, walk 2 min, repeat 5
SUNDAY	**REST DAY**

2ND WEEK EXERCISE PLAN

MONDAY	• 25 squats, 1 min rest, repeat 2x • 30 sec plank, 1 min rest, repeat 3x • 25 crunches, 1 min rest, repeat 4x • 20 lunges, 1 min rest, repeat 2x • 30 sec walls sit, 1 min rest, repeat 3x • 12 pushups, 1 min rest, repeat 2x • 2x judo roll with jump, 10 sec rest, repeat 10x • 10 1-pound weights lift, 30 sec rest, repeat 4x each hand • Jogging with high knees for 2 min • Run fast 2 min, walk 2 min, repeat 6x
TUSEDAY	• 20 squat thrusters, 1 min rest, repeat 2x • 50 sec plank, 1 min rest, repeat 2x • 20 lunges, 1 min rest, repeat 2x • 10x reverse lunge, 1 min rest, repeat 2x • 10 plyo-pushups, 1 min rest, repeat 2x • 10 2-pound weights lift, 1 min rest, repeat 4x each hand • 10 side to side jumping lunges, 1 min rest, repeat 2x • 10 hip raises with 1-pound weighs around the ankle, 1 min rest, repeat 3x each side • Run for 25 min
WEDNESDAY	REST DAY
THURSTDAY	• 25 squats, 1 min rest, repeat 4x • 35 sec plank, 1 min rest, repeat 2x • 20 crunches, 1 min rest, repeat 3x • 10 long jumps, 1 min rest, repeat 2x • 12x reverse lunge, 1 min rest, repeat 2x • 2x judo roll with jump, 10 sec rest, repeat 10x • 10 sit ups, 1 min rest, repeat 4x • 10 speed skaters with 1-pound weights, 1 min rest, repeat 2x • 10 2-pound weights lift, 1 min rest, repeat 4x each hand • Jogging with high knees for 2 min • Run fast 2 min, walk 2 min, repeat 8x
FRIDAY	• 30 squats, 1 min rest, repeat 5x • 1 min plank, 2 min rest, repeat 2x • 30 crunches, 1 min rest, repeat 4x • 2x judo roll with jump, 10 sec rest, repeat 10x • 40 sec walls sit, 1 min rest, repeat 2x • 10 sit ups, 1 min rest, repeat 4x • 12 jumping jacks, 15 sec rest, repeat 4x • 10 side to side jumping lunges, 1 min rest, repeat 2x • 10 mountain climbers, 1 min rest, repeat 2x

	• 10 2-pound weights lift, 1 min rest, repeat 6x each hand • 10 hip raises with 1-pound weighs around the ankle, 1 min rest, repeat 3x each side • Run fast 2 min, walk 2 min, repeat 8x
SATHURDAY	**REST DAY**
SUNDAY	• 20 squats, 1 min rest, repeat 2x • 1 min plank, 1 min rest, repeat 2x • 10 plyo-pushups, 1 min rest, repeat 4x • 2x judo roll with jump, 10 sec rest, repeat 10x • 20 crunches, 1 min rest, repeat 3x • 10 jumping jacks, 15 sec rest, repeat 4x • 50 sec walls sit, 1 min rest, repeat 2x • 10 pushups, 1 min rest, repeat 2x • 25 sit ups, 1 min rest, repeat 2x • 10 mountain climbers, 1 min rest, repeat 4x • 10 side to side jumping lunges, 1 min rest, repeat 2x • 10 2-pound weights lift, 1 min rest, repeat 6x each hand • 10 hip raises with 1-pound weighs around the ankle, 1 min rest, repeat 3x each side • Run fast 2 min, walk 2 min, repeat 10x

3RD WEEK EXERCISE PLAN

MONDAY	REST DAY
TUSEDAY	• 20 squat thrusters, 1 min rest, repeat 2x • 50 sec plank, 1 min rest, repeat 4x • 20 lunges, 1 min rest, repeat 2x • 10x reverse lunge, 1 min rest, repeat 4x • 10 plyo-pushups, 1 min rest, repeat 4x • 10 2-pound weights lift, 1 min rest, repeat 6x each hand • 10 side to side jumping lunges, 1 min rest, repeat 4x • 10 hip raises with 1-pound weighs around the ankle, 1 min rest, repeat 4x each side • 4x judo roll with jump, 10 sec rest, repeat 4x • Run fast 2 min, walk 2 min, repeat 8x
TUESDAY	• 30 squats, 1 min rest, repeat 4x • 1 min plank, 2 min rest, repeat 4x • 30 crunches, 1 min rest, repeat 4x • 15 long jumps, 1 min rest, repeat 4x • 12x reverse lunge, 1 min rest, repeat 4x • 4x judo roll with jump, 10 sec rest, repeat 6x • 10 jumping jacks, 30 sec rest, repeat 4x • 10 sit ups, 1 min rest, repeat 4x • 10 2-pound weights lift, 1 min rest, repeat 4x each hand • 10 hip raises with 1-pound weighs around the ankle, 1 min rest, repeat 4x each side • Run fast 2 min, walk 2 min, repeat 10x
WEDNESDAY	REST DAY
FRIDAY	• 1 min plank, 2 min rest, repeat 4x • 2x judo roll with jump, 10 sec rest, repeat 4x • 20 jumping jacks, 30 sec rest, repeat 4x • 10 speed skaters with 1-pound weights, 1 min rest, repeat 2x • 10 side to side jumping lunges, 1 min rest, repeat 2x • 30 crunches, 1 min rest, repeat 4x • Jogging with high knees for 2 min • 10 2-pound weights lift, 1 min rest, repeat 6x each hand • Run fast 2 min, walk 2 min, repeat 20x
SATHURDAY	• 20 jumping squats, 1 min rest, repeat 4x • 1 min plank, 1 min rest, repeat 2x • 12 plyo-pushups, 1 min rest, repeat 4x • 2x judo roll with jump, 10 sec rest, repeat 2x • 30 crunches, 1 min rest, repeat 4x • 20 jumping jacks, 30 sec rest, repeat 4x • 1 min walls sit, 1 min rest, repeat 2x • 12 pushups, 1 min rest, repeat 2x

285

	• 25 sit ups, 1 min rest, repeat 2x
	• 12 mountain climbers, 1 min rest, repeat 4x
	• 15 side to side jumping lunges, 1 min rest, repeat 2x
	• 10 2-pound weights lift, 1 min rest, repeat 6x each hand
	• 20 speed skaters with 2-pound weights, 1 min rest, repeat 2x
	• 10 hip raises with 2-pound weighs around the ankle, 1 min rest, repeat 4x each side
	• Run for 20 min, walk for 2 min, repeat 2x
SUNDAY	**REST DAY**

4ᵀᴴ WEEK EXERCISE PLAN

MONDAY	• 30 prisoner squat jumps, 1 min rest, repeat 4x • 1 min plank, 30 sec rest, repeat 4x • 15 long jumps, 30 sec rest, repeat 4x • 15 reverse lunges, 1 min rest, repeat 4x • 15 plyo-pushups, 1 min rest, repeat 4x • 4x judo roll with jump, 10 sec rest, repeat 4x • 20 2-pound weights lift, 1 min rest, repeat 6x each hand • 20 speed skaters with 2-pound weights, 1 min rest, repeat 2x • 15 side to side jumping lunges, 1 min rest, repeat 4x • 15 hip raises with 2-pound weighs around the ankle, 1 min rest, repeat 4x each side • Jogging with high knees for 4 min • Run for 20 min, walk 2 min, repeat 2x
TUSEDAY	• 20 squat thrusters, 1 min rest, repeat 2x • 50 sec plank, 1 min rest, repeat 4x • 20 lunges, 1 min rest, repeat 2x • 10x reverse lunge, 1 min rest, repeat 4x • 10 plyo-pushups, 1 min rest, repeat 4x • 10 2-pound weights lift, 1 min rest, repeat 6x each hand • 10 side to side jumping lunges, 1 min rest, repeat 4x • 10 hip raises with 1-pound weighs around the ankle, 1 min rest, repeat 4x each side • 10 speed skaters with 2-pound weights, 1 min rest, repeat 2x • 4x judo roll with jump, 10 sec rest, repeat 4x • Run fast 2 min, walk 2 min, repeat 10x
WEDNESDAY	• 30 squats, 1 min rest, repeat 4x • 1 min plank, 2 min rest, repeat 4x • 30 crunches, 1 min rest, repeat 4x • 15 long jumps, 1 min rest, repeat 4x • 12x reverse lunge, 1 min rest, repeat 4x • 4x judo roll with jump, 10 sec rest, repeat 6x • 10 jumping jacks, 30 sec rest, repeat 4x • 12 sit ups, 1 min rest, repeat 4x • 12 2-pound weights lift, 1 min rest, repeat 4x each hand • 12 hip raises with 1-pound weighs around the ankle, 1 min rest, repeat 4x each side • Run fast 2 min, walk 2 min, repeat 20x
THURSTDAY	**REST DAY**
	• 30 squats, 1 min rest, repeat 6x • 1 min plank, 2 min rest, repeat 4x • 2x judo roll with jump, 10 sec rest, repeat 4x

287

FRIDAY	• 25 jumping jacks, 30 sec rest, repeat 4x • 15 side to side jumping lunges, 1 min rest, repeat 2x • 30 crunches, 1 min rest, repeat 4x • 20 speed skaters with 2-pound weights, 1 min rest, repeat 2x • Jogging with high knees for 6 min • 10 2-pound weights lift, 1 min rest, repeat 6x each hand • Run fast 2 min, walk 2 min, repeat 10x
SATHURDAY	• 30 jumping squats, 1 min rest, repeat 4x • 1 min plank, 1 min rest, repeat 2x • 10 plyo-pushups, 1 min rest, repeat 4x • 2x judo roll with jump, 10 sec rest, repeat 2x • 30 crunches, 1 min rest, repeat 4x • 20 jumping jacks, 30 sec rest, repeat 4x • 1 min walls sit, 1 min rest, repeat 2x • 12 pushups, 1 min rest, repeat 2x • 25 sit ups, 1 min rest, repeat 2x • 12 mountain climbers, 1 min rest, repeat 4x • Jogging with high knees for 4 min • 15 side to side jumping lunges, 1 min rest, repeat 3x • 10 2-pound weights lift, 1 min rest, repeat 6x each hand • 10 hip raises with 2-pound weighs around the ankle, 1 min rest, repeat 4x each side • Run fast 2 min, walk 2 min, repeat 20
SUNDAY	**REST DAY**